FOCUS ON IMPACT

D0830617

Praise for Focus On Impact

"Wendy Lipton-Dibner is the master of impact strategy. Her newest book, *Focus On Impact* is a critical tool for the rapidly-changing global market. Well-written, practical and smart. A must-read."

—**Harvey MacKay,** #1 *New York Times* bestselling author,
Swim With The Sharks Without Being Eaten Alive

"Wendy Lipton-Dibner's *Focus On Impact* presents a powerful and actionable roadmap for monetizing your impact in the 21st century. A must-read for entrepreneurs, executives and non-profit leaders."

—**Bob Proctor,** bestselling author, *The ABC's of Success,*
Chairman & Co-Founder, Proctor Gallagher Institute

"My father asked me every night, 'Sharon, have you impacted someone's life for good today?' That simple question has been the guiding light for my life. In *Focus On Impact*, Wendy Lipton-Dibner has created the authoritative thesis for creating positive impact in the lives of others—each and every day! This action guide will support you in transforming your life from where you are today to the life of your dreams through re-focusing your actions from creating financial success to creating positive impact on, and for others. By changing your focus, not only are you creating a better life for yourself and others, you will also see the financial rewards as a result of the impact you make."

—**Sharon Lechter, CPA CGMA,**
bestselling author, *Think and Grow Rich for Women,* co-author,
Outwitting the Devil, Three Feet from Gold and *Rich Dad Poor Dad*

"This masterfully written guidebook gives you the step-by-step to build a sustainable and profitable difference in the world."

—**Greg S. Reid**, author of the *Think and Grow Rich* series

"If gaining clear insight is the first key to success, Wendy's latest book, *Focus On Impact*, is an absolute necessity. Don't just read it. Work through it to find your clear path to amazing fulfillment in all areas of your life."

—**Tom Hopkins**, author, *When Buyers Say No*

"Wendy Lipton-Dibner's *Focus On Impact* is the next business milestone. Filled with original thinking and backed up by proof and practicality, this book is a powerful tool for creating profitable relationships in any market."

—**John Gray, PhD**, *New York Times* bestselling author, *Men Are From Mars, Women Are From Venus* and *Conscious Men*

"I can recall when *Chicken Soup for the Soul* launched to legendary record setting global success. Then came *The Secret, Mars and Venus, No Matter What, Three Feet From Gold, Rich Dad Poor Dad, Outwitting the Devil* and *Think & Grow Rich for Women*. All readers of these books MUST read *Focus On Impact* as the final work to transform your personal and professional goal attainment. All you finally need is *Focus On Impact* to win more fully. Spread the word of our major endorsement for *Focus On Impact*. Tony Robbins, read this ONE!"

—**Berny Dohrmann,** Founder, CEO Space, International

"Capitalize on the new economy and future-proof your business with Wendy Lipton-Dibner's newest how-to masterpiece, *Focus On Impact*. Her book contains some of the best strategies I've seen in a long time, with practical application for new and thriving enterprises in all industries. It's a brilliant approach. Read it, use it, share it."

—**Cheryl Snapp Conner**, CEO SnappConner PR, author, *Beyond PR: Communication Like a Champ in the Digital Age*, contributor to Forbes.com.

"If you want to make an unstoppable difference in the world that lets you live the life you want while growing your business, you've got to read *Focus On Impact*. Wendy Lipton-Dibner's unique business model is ideal for entrepreneurs and non-profit leaders who are driven to increase their global footprint with measurable results."

—**Cynthia Kersey**, Founder and CEO, Unstoppable Foundation and member of the Transformational Leadership Council

"If you think it's all been said already, then you need to read *Focus On Impact*. This powerful book is filled with one-of-a-kind strategies that make business fun, fulfilling and profitable. Grow your success with the difference-maker who's been there, done that and is doing it bigger every year. Wendy Lipton-Dibner will take you wherever you want to go!"

—**Rick Frishman**, international bestselling author, CEO, Planned TV Arts and Founder, Author 101 University

"Smart executives and savvy entrepreneurs maintain a competitive edge by tracking trends and implementing best practices. Wendy Lipton-Dibner's newest book, *Focus On Impact*, presents a goldmine of unique business growth strategies and practical formulas that you simply can't afford to ignore. Read it, use it like a GPS and become a significant point of influence and success."

—**Stefan Swanepoel**, *New York Times* bestselling author, Chairman and CEO, Swanepoel T3 Group of Companies

"Wendy Lipton-Dibner has done it again! In the ground-breaking *Focus On Impact*, Wendy describes impact as 'the new global currency.' I couldn't agree more. Wendy's approach to achieving 'impact' is thoughtful, introspective, stimulating, and very practical. Many consultants and content experts avoid the territory of personal values as this can be a minefield. But Wendy addresses this head-on, and discusses the source of a person's deeply held value system. Once that is understood, a person's impact can be guided for personal success. With a voice of compassion and teaching, Wendy's concepts are strategies that the reader/leader can begin implementing immediately—and success and profit will follow."

—**Nancy Collins**, President and Publisher, *The Journal of Medical Practice Management*, Greenbranch Publishing, Phoenix, MD

See ***More Praise for Focus On Impact*** on Page 170

FOCUS ON
IMPACT

THE 10-STEP MAP TO
REACH MILLIONS, MAKE MILLIONS
AND LOVE YOUR LIFE
ALONG THE WAY

Wendy Lipton-Dibner

New York

A free eBook edition is available
with the purchase of this print book.

CLEARLY PRINT YOUR NAME ABOVE IN UPPER CASE

Instructions to claim your free eBook edition:
1. Download the BitLit app for Android or iOS
2. Write your name in **UPPER CASE** on the line
3. Use the BitLit app to submit a photo
4. Download your eBook to any device

In an effort to support local communities and raise awareness and funds, Morgan James Publishing donates a percentage of all book sales for the life of each book to Habitat for Humanity Peninsula and Greater Williamsburg.

Get involved today, visit
www.MorganJamesBuilds.com

FOCUS ON IMPACT®
THE 10-STEP MAP TO REACH MILLIONS, MAKE MILLIONS AND LOVE YOUR LIFE ALONG THE WAY

© 2016 Professional Impact, Inc.

No portion of this book may be reproduced, stored in a retrieval system or transmitted in any form or by any means—electronic, mechanical, photocopy, recording, scanning or otherwise, except for brief quotations in critical reviews or articles, without the prior written permission of Professional Impact, Inc.

FOCUS ON IMPACT is a registered trademark of Professional Impact, Inc.

Disclaimer: This book, including any portion thereof, is not intended to offer any legal, professional, personal or financial advice. The information contained herein does not replace or substitute for the services of trained professionals in any field, including, but not limited to, financial or legal services. Under no circumstances will Professional Impact, Inc. or any of its officers, directors, representatives, agents, affiliates or contractors be liable for any special or consequential damages that are associated with the use of, or the inability to use, the information or strategies communicated through this book, even if advised of the possibility of such damages. You alone are responsible and accountable for your decisions, actions and results in life and by your use of this book, you agree not to attempt to hold us liable for any such decisions, actions or results, at any time, under any circumstance.

We've taken every effort to ensure we accurately represent these strategies and their potential to help you grow your business. However, we do not purport this as a "get rich scheme" and there is no guarantee that you will earn any money using the techniques discussed in this book. This book is provided for information only and no guarantees, promises, representations or warranties of any kind regarding specific or general benefits, monetary or otherwise, have been or will be made by us. Your level of success in attaining similar results is dependent upon a number of factors including your skill, knowledge, ability, dedication, personality, market, business savvy, business focus, business goals, partners and financial situation. Because these factors differ according to individuals, including their circumstances and efforts, we cannot guarantee your success, income level or ability to earn revenue and specifically do not make any such representations. Any forward-looking or financial statements outlined in this book, or in any materials or statements disseminated by us in any way are simply our expectations or forecasts for future potential and thus are not promises for actual performance. These statements are simply derived from our opinion and/or experience. We make no guarantees that you will achieve any particular results from our information and we are not responsible for your actions and results in business or in life.

Published in New York, New York, by Morgan James Publishing. Morgan James and The Entrepreneurial Publisher are trademarks of Morgan James, LLC.
www.MorganJamesPublishing.com

The Morgan James Speakers Group can bring authors to your live event. For more information or to book an event visit The Morgan James Speakers Group at www.TheMorganJamesSpeakersGroup.com.

ISBN 978-1-63047-402-7 paperback
ISBN 978-1-63047-332-7 eBook
Library of Congress Control Number: 2014959668

Cover Design: Foster Covers

Also by Wendy Lipton-Dibner

Shatter Your Speed Limits®

M.A.D. Leadership For Healthcare™

The Expert Success Solution Volume 1

The Expert Success Solution Volume 2

Seminars by Wendy Lipton-Dibner

Move People To Action™

Difference-Maker Summit™

Elite Video Mastery™

Meet Wendy online and receive free training at:

www.ProfessionalImpact.com

IMPACT is the measurable difference you create in people's lives as the direct result of contact with you, your team and your company's message, marketing, products and services.

This book is dedicated to the difference-makers.

CONTENTS

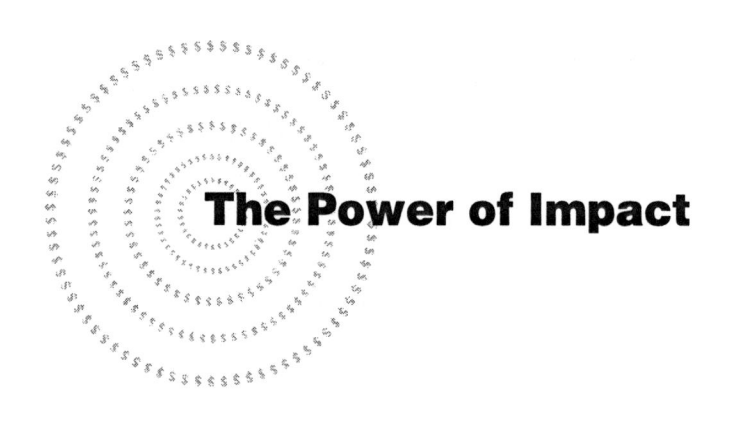

The Power of Impact

I believe we are all born with amazing powers and the greatest power of all is our ability to make an impact on people's lives.

You've been using your power to impact people since the first moment you moved inside your mother's womb. With one little kick, you touched the very core of her being and moved her to think, feel and act in ways she'd never done before.

And ever since that first moment of impact, you've touched hundreds, maybe even thousands of lives—simply by being you and interacting with people.

Every email, every text, every post, every tweet, the simple act of ordering a cup of coffee, answering your phone or smiling at a stranger…

Everything you do and everything you *don't* do has an impact on someone else—and when you purposefully infuse your unique impact into your message, products and services, that's when you'll see its greatest power.

As a pebble creates ripples in a pond, moving further and further from the point of origin, so will your impact spread far beyond your reach. Make your impact *measurable* and the vast majority of people you'll touch over the course of your entire life will be people you'll never meet! Because when you impact just one person, s/he will change in some way and then carry your impact on to someone else. And your ripple will move on, with one person touching another in an endless cycle of impact.

The more effective your impact, the more it will stretch around the globe and extend far into the future touching generations yet unborn.

That is the power of impact. And it all begins with you. You were born with the amazing power to make a unique impact on people's lives and I believe life's most important journey is discovering how you're going to use this powerful gift—before it's too late and you miss your chance.

I'm writing this book because I want you to have the formulas you need to make the greatest impact possible.

So let's do this. Because the world needs your impact now. And because life is far too short to settle for less than you truly want—in your business or your life.

Thank you for giving me the privilege of guiding you on your Journey of Impact.

Wendy

Preface

Now is the Time

Never before in history has there been a greater opportunity for impact-driven entrepreneurs, experts and executives than right now.

If you have a message, a product or a service that can help people live better lives, now is the perfect time to maximize and capitalize on your impact.

Why now?

Today's consumers are more cynical, skeptical and cautious than ever before. They've learned the hard way that just because you *say* you can help them, doesn't mean you will. They've learned to do their research, to seek out the opinions of friends and strangers and to say *"no"* rather than risk the disappointment, humiliation or danger of poor choices.

These consumers have learned to take full advantage of the *Era of Entitlement*—a time unlike any in history when they have easy access to a plethora of free information, free entertainment, free vacations, free

xv

books, free training, free consulting, free healthcare, free apps, and free samples of just about any product or service—all with a single click anywhere, anytime, on any device.

So how do you capitalize on the new economy? Focus On Impact!

Impact is the new global currency.

Whether you're just starting out or you're the CEO of a multinational company, now is the time to Focus On Impact.

Your unique impact is your strongest ally in every market, no matter your message, product or service. It opens doors to strategic alliances, extraordinary adventures and abundant rewards.

Impact lets you enjoy wealth guilt-free, knowing the money that buys your lifestyle is the direct result of the difference you're making in the world.

Impact is your golden ticket into the hearts and homes of consumers of any demographic you want to reach.

Impact takes you from *Who are you?* to *What credit cards do you accept?* without ever doing a pushy sales presentation.

Impact is what people want. And if you've got a passion for making a difference, that is very good news for you.

No one can capitalize on this economy better than someone who is driven to make a difference in people's lives.

Today's world is the perfect platform for you as billions of people search online, waiting for your impact to appear. So how do you get those people to find you, follow you, choose you, buy from you and send all their friends to your door? Follow the *Focus On Impact Map*.

The *Focus On Impact Map* is the only, step-by-step, comprehensive model ever created, tested and proven to build and grow businesses that produce products and services that make a measurable difference in people's lives.

The success of the Focus On Impact Map has been proven around the globe in booming economies and deep recessions. It provides step-by-step strategic sequencing, clarity-producing formulas and practical solutions that have been shown to be effective across a vast array of industries, products and services.

You can use the Focus On Impact Map whether you're on your own or serving with a massive team. It enables you to capitalize on what I call *Impact Strategy.*

Impact Strategy is the process of combining proven science[1] with ethical business growth formulas[2] to create, market and deliver one-of-a-kind products and services that make a measurable difference in people's lives.

Impact Strategy formulas make it possible for you to easily identify, maximize and monetize your unique difference while optimizing your freedom and flexibility as you build and grow your success. The formulas become even stronger when used within the Focus On Impact Map.

I originally developed Impact Strategy and the Focus On Impact Map while building my first business. The power of this strategic model made it possible for me to grow with unprecedented speed and results. In fact, as soon as local merchants saw the rapid success of my business, they began inviting me to speak at local business meetings held by the Chamber of Commerce, Rotary® and other groups. As I shared some of the key formulas I'd used to grow my business, I discovered the success of these formulas wasn't exclusive to my business—their power was transferrable to others who used them effectively.

Since then, I've used the Focus On Impact Map to build 10 successful retail and service businesses of my own. Along the way I've shared

---

1   Sociology, social psychology, clinical psychology, anthropology, biology and neuropsychology.

2   I define "ethical" as the process of being ever vigilant to assure the impact we bring to people's lives through our marketing, products and services is designed to help them get what they want without causing physical, financial or emotional harm.

many of my formulas through multiple bestselling books, hundreds of media appearances and thousands of keynote presentations on stages around the globe. I've had the honor of serving a wide variety of clients, including multi-national sales and manufacturing corporations, public utilities, educational institutions, hospitals, private medical, dental, wellness, legal and financial practices, non-profit organizations, retail chains, small businesses, entrepreneurs, mompreneurs, MLM leaders, and a vast array of speakers, authors, coaches, consultants and top influencers.[3]

Through it all, I always followed the Focus On Impact Map, updating my Impact Strategy formulas as needed to accommodate changes in the global economy.

The model you're about to discover is precisely what I've used to grow my own businesses and to help my clients maximize and capitalize on their impact.

While I became known worldwide as a leading authority in business and personal development, I'd never revealed the complete Focus On Impact Map to anyone until I accepted an invitation to speak at an entrepreneurial conference. My host's request was specific:

"Give us a 90-minute training that will have something actionable for everyone from Start-Ups to Fortune 100 CEOs."[4]

I'm a social researcher by training and passion, so two months prior to the engagement, I attended one of their conferences and interviewed the 200+ entrepreneurs in attendance. I also conducted a random survey of my own community, yielding a total of nearly 1000 respondents representing a wide array of business acumen and experience.

The data clearly revealed what was missing for these difference-makers:

---

3   I'm not going to distract you now with my life story. If you're interested, it's available for you in **Meet Wendy** on Page 181.

4   I'll be forever grateful to Berny Dohrmann, founder of CEO Space International for providing me the inspiration and privilege of revealing my Focus On Impact Map for the first time on his stage. Meet Berny at www.FocusOnImpact.com/resources.

✓ **Clarity** of vision and operationalization so their ideas could be translated into measurable results;

✓ **Consecutive Sequencing** to create optimal outcomes while minimizing time and expense;

✓ **Comprehensive Strategies** to identify, maximize and capitalize on their impact;

✓ **Customization** so they could use proven formulas without compromising their personal and professional uniqueness;

✓ **Collaboration** with other difference-makers to increase reach and revenues exponentially; and

✓ **Community** to support them along the way.

There was no doubt I had the solution for these success-seekers. They needed my complete Focus On Impact Map. But…

It's one thing to have proven solutions…
It's quite another to reveal them to the world.

The Focus On Impact Map was the foundation of my business, my proprietary process, my *secret sauce!* Why would I give it away?

Because if 1000 difference-makers aren't getting their impact out effectively, that means there are more like them who are struggling to get their messages, products and services seen and enjoyed. And *that* means there are men, women and children worldwide who can't access the unique help only these people can provide.

I thought about my corporate mission:

Our mission is to make an impact on people's lives so
they in turn can make an impact on every life they touch.

As long as I held onto my secret, I was limiting the impact of others and not living up to my mission.

It was time to pass the baton…

On August 21, 2014, the stage manager pulled back the curtain and offered his hand for me to step up onto the stage. My eyes filled with tears as the audience rose to their feet in applause. Standing in front of me were entrepreneurs who could shape the future with their impact. I saw their hopeful smiles and felt deeply humbled to be serving them.

They interrupted my presentation frequently with spontaneous applause, whoops of joy and more than a few tears as I walked them step-by-step through my Focus On Impact Map. I'd given them a super-sized handout of the Map and barely saw the whites of their eyes as they filled the page edge-to-edge with notes. It was an extraordinary launch of what has become a passion-filled journey to spread this information to every difference-maker worldwide on stages, online and in media.

And now here you are, holding my complete Map in your hands. That's what happens when you Focus On Impact.

What kind of success can you build when you Focus On Impact? That's entirely up to you! Here are some examples:

- ✓ Start a new business and get paid for the impact you bring the world
- ✓ Drive more of the right customers to your local retail and/or service business
- ✓ Release your next Annual Report with celebratory pride (and relief!)
- ✓ Increase referral-based sales in your local, national and international markets
- ✓ Attract and engage your perfect market online and offline
- ✓ Get people to click, like, buy and share without sleazy sales tactics
- ✓ Build funds and awareness for your charitable organization
- ✓ Make a greater difference and capitalize with MLM teams
- ✓ Share your life lessons through speaking and bestselling books
- ✓ Get more clients for your coaching or consulting business
- ✓ Get off the low-reimbursement treadmill by building a healthcare practice that's right for you
- ✓ Develop your reputation as a top influencer across multiple industries

✓ Ethically generate extra money so you can spoil your grandchildren
✓ Maximize "Impact Investing" results by giving the Focus On Impact Map to everyone you support
✓ Finally get what you truly want—for your business and your life!

Whether you want to make your impact locally, nationally or internationally... in your kitchen, a skyscraper or traveling the world...

There is no limit to the opportunities that await you when you Focus On Impact.

I'm so excited you're finally going to have the information you need so you can convert your ideas into impact and your impact into revenue by systematically building your business within a structure that gives you the freedom to be who you are and live a life you love.

It's time to take total control over the shape of your impact, the size of your impact and the rewards you receive as a result of your impact.

Your desire to make a difference in the world will be your best asset in this economy and the Focus On Impact Map will be your strongest ally.

Now turn the page and let's do this together!

How to Get the Most From This Book

It's one thing to buy a book.
It's another to read it.
It's everything when you implement it.

There is a timeless truth in business: *Success only comes to those who put in the work.* The question is: what kind of *work* will you put in? In my experience, the *work* of building and managing an impact-driven business is wonderfully joyous when it is customized to your uniqueness, reflects your purpose and actually succeeds.

I believe success is not measured by the money we make but by the number of people we serve and the joy we experience making it happen. As it turns out, I'm not the only one who holds this belief, nor am I the only person to prosper from it. In fact, the most successful, sustainable businesses have historically been those whose products and services were designed to make a difference in people's lives.

WHO CAN SUCCEED WITH THIS BOOK?

The secret to building your success is to identify your unique impact and package it in a way that helps you reach all the people you want to serve so they click, like, buy, use and share everything you create while you enjoy every step of your Journey of Impact.

This book will help you make all of that happen as long as your primary goal is to make a difference in people's lives.[5]

If your primary objective is to get rich, the Focus On Impact Map will probably not work for you. However, if your goal is to get rich *as a result of* your impact, you're in the right place!

The Focus On Impact Map will help you succeed if you follow the sequence in order, apply the strategies effectively and consistently, and if you are in one of the following groups:

1) Start-Up Transitioner

You've been living your life and now you want to transition into something new—ideally, something that will enable you to make a difference, leave a lasting legacy, make enough money so you can stop thinking about money and provide plenty of flexibility to put it all aside when family and friends need you to be there for them. You may not be sure about what you want to do or how to do it, but you're itching for something new that will challenge you, fulfill you and give you the freedom to live your life as you choose while you build your new business.

2) Passionate Messenger

You have an important message to share with the world and you've been actively trying to find a way to get it out. You'd like to get paid to speak, publish a bestselling book, get invited for media interviews and produce products and/or services to help people. Your friends and family think you're a little crazy for trying to do this, but you're driven to make your difference and would do it all for free if you could just

---

5   My research has shown time again: People who focus on money never make as much money with my strategies as do those who Focus On Impact.

make enough money to know your family is secure. You've attended seminars, teleseminars and webinars, listened to podcasts, MP3s and CDs, purchased online courses, DVDs and coaching programs, and your shelves and devices are filled with self-help, motivation and business books. You've learned a lot, but you're still not getting your message out or making the impact you know you can make. Your passion keeps driving you forward—but you're running out of time and money.

3) Small Business Owner

You've been in business for at least a year and, while you've made progress, you're not where you'd like to be. You've gotten caught up in the day-to-day details and now you feel like you just need a better plan—something that will make sure you're heading in the right direction, help you stay on course and bring your business where you want it to go without getting sidetracked by all the ideas everyone has for you about how to succeed. You're looking for guidance, strategy, practical tips and validation that you really have what it takes to make this happen.

4) Results-Driven Entrepreneur

You've been involved in one or more successful businesses, you've brought multiple products and services to market, and you're respected for your results-driven approach to getting things done. You're always looking for fresh ideas to increase and accelerate your growth, reinvigorate your team and sharpen your edge. You're actively seeking alternative perspectives and proven strategies to maximize multiple areas of your business and capitalize on the success you've already built while keeping yourself open for opportunities that come along.

5) Non-Profit Leader

Your cause is strong, your volunteers are driven and your board is supportive. But when everyone else goes home, it's you sitting at your desk trying to figure out a plan that will raise funds and awareness without burning out your team or your donors. You look at the retail parking lots filled with cars, so you know people are spending. That tells you the secret to making this work is to use proven business strategies, but they all seem sleazy and inappropriate for your impact-driven mission. Still, you're actively looking for a strategic plan to get more people engaged in your mission and to show their support with donations.

6) Executive Maverick

You get it. The game has changed and everyone is talking about impact. CEOs are smiling into video cameras, doing their best to look compassionate and sound authentic while they talk about social responsibility and their commitment to their customers. You get it. You also get that behind closed doors, the conversations are about profitability, cost reduction and ROI. Your instincts are telling you to get on top of this impact thing and that it should be easy since your products and services really do make a difference in people's lives. You're determined to find a way to maximize and capitalize on what you've got sitting right in front of you. But to get it done, you're going to need something concrete—a tactical strategy you can use with practical steps your team can take to bring exponential growth without coloring too far outside the lines.

Find your fit? Great! Let's keep going…

3 STEPS TO MAXIMIZE AND CAPITALIZE

Whether you're a bottom-line person or savor the details, for maximum results, follow these three steps:

Step 1: Read Each Chapter in Order

Like any map, if you go out of sequence, you're likely to get lost, hit unexpected road hazards and miss your exit. Simply follow the Focus On Impact Map and your journey will be much more enjoyable and significantly more profitable![6]

---

6   While each chapter stands on its own, each is built upon the step(s) before. Even if you've been in business for many years, I recommend you start at the beginning and walk through each step in sequence. Somewhere in this book is at least one piece you've been missing to take your business further.

Step 2: Accelerate with the Action Steps

At the end of each chapter you'll find targeted Action Steps to help you move forward faster and avoid being overwhelmed. To fully capitalize, read the entire book through once, then begin again, quickly review each chapter and follow the instructions provided in the associated Action Steps.

Step 3: Join the Community

If you get stuck, help is just a click away at Facebook.com/focusonimpact. There you'll find the Community of Difference-Makers™—people who Focus On Impact and who will support you along the way. Simply LIKE the page, post "*I'm ready!*" and we will welcome you with open arms. I am active in the Community and look forward to meeting you there so I can help you capitalize on *your* Focus On Impact Map!

IS THIS BOOK ALL YOU NEED?

I have no way of knowing the answer to that question. Your unique situation and experience will dictate what you need and what you'll accomplish.

Your impact is really important to me, so I'm packing everything I can fit into these pages and then I'll show you where to get complimentary Impact Gifts from me all year long, including discounted access to online training and my live events.

Why is your impact so important to me? Because all around the world, billions of people are desperately searching for products and services that will help them get free from their pain and bring more joy into their lives. These people are scared for their families, for the future of generations to come and for the safety of our planet. They're looking for help because 1) they know they can't do it alone and 2) up to this point, they haven't been able to find the help they need. These people have been searching for their difference-maker(s), but no one has been the right fit for them.

Just as every pot has a unique lid that will fit snuggly, every person has a unique difference-maker that's just the right fit for his/her needs.

And when that difference-maker provides just the right impact in just the right way at just the right moment with just the right message, products and services—that's when it all comes together.

As you read this book, billions of people are searching (online and off) for solutions to their problems and here's what makes that important for you:

People are searching because their problems haven't been solved. Why? Because they haven't yet found the right lid for their pot! [7]

Your impact will grow exponentially the moment you discover how to be the right lid for the people you want to serve and send your impact out to them in a way that connects for them. That's when people will trust you and listen to you and follow your advice and pay top fees for your products and services. I'm going to show you how to make it all happen in this book, but here's the bottom line:

People can't afford to wait while you try to figure out how to get your impact into their lives. The clock is ticking and the Focus On Impact Map is the shortest distance between them and you.

All I have to do is show you how to identify and maximize your unique impact and use it to help people *find you, follow you and choose you so they'll buy what you create, use what they buy, get measurable results, tell all their friends and come back for more.*

All *you* need to do is take my hand, Focus On Impact and follow the Map. If you're willing to do that, then I will show you precisely how to use it.

I won't promise it will be easy—challenging the status quo is never easy. But I will promise you this:

---

7   In case you've never heard the expression, "*There's a lid for every pot*" is a cooking metaphor. Picture this: You're getting ready to cook pasta so you pull out a pot and a lid. You grab the wrong lid and when you place it on the pot it just drops down to the bottom. You fish it out and try another, but it's way too big. Now you start pulling out every lid you've got until finally you find the right lid—the perfect fit for your pot. And voilà! Perfect pasta! This is one of the most important keys to capitalizing on the power of impact: Be their lid!

If you'll believe in yourself only half as much as I believe in you, then together our impact will be far greater than either of us will ever make alone.

It's been said, *"Every journey begins with a single step."*

Your next step is to turn the page...

Chapter One

The Multimillion-Dollar Mindset

There are two types of businesses: those that focus on making money and those that focus on making a measurable impact in people's lives. Guess which type makes more money.

W hen I was a senior in high school, I took an economics class that forever changed my perspective on business. The entire semester was devoted to helping us understand business from the inside out through field research. Each student was assigned four businesses in our local area ranging from family-owned restaurants and franchise owners to publicly held multi-national corporations and healthcare practices.

Our assignment was clear: Explain how each business makes money.

Over the course of that semester I interviewed owners, executives, employees and customers while observing day-to-day operations in every aspect of each business, all in search of the secret path to the money.

1

While my four subjects vastly differed in products and services, they all shared a primary goal: to maximize profitability. They accomplished their goal by making sure everything they did, from product development to customer service, minimized expenses and maximized sales.

Every aspect of their business was focused on money.

Not one of those businesses increased revenues in the time I studied them, nor do they exist today. In fact, my career has shown focusing on money is the worst thing you can do if your goal is to make a significant difference in the world and reap substantial rewards as a result.

Don't get me wrong. I love money. Money is security. Money is luxury. Money is power. Money is freedom. Money is fun!

But is it smart business to *focus* on money? My high school economics teacher would have said, *YES!* And with all respect to him and all who hold traditional business mindsets, I'm here to tell you,

When you focus on money, you have to invest significantly more money to make up for the problems you caused by focusing on money.

I've conducted hundreds of organizational research and evaluation studies, consulted for and trained well-over one thousand corporate, healthcare, small business and non-profit organizations and surveyed well-over 500,000 experts, executives and entrepreneurs who sat in my audiences around the globe. Without exception, the results have consistently shown:

Traditional business models don't work for difference-makers.

Okay, so the question you might be asking is,

What is a difference-maker?

A difference-maker is someone who has a message, product or service that can help others live happier, healthier, easier, more productive, safer, longer, more fulfilling, less stressful, more exciting, less boring, more loving, more vibrant, more functional, less lonely, more satisfying, or more joyful lives.

Difference-makers are found in multi-national corporations, hospitals, private practices, non-profit organizations and small businesses around the globe. They're sitting in the bleachers at high school soccer games and in cars waiting for fast-food burgers. They are the thinkers, dreamers, creators, speakers, authors, bloggers, engineers, teachers, leaders, influencers, entertainers, clergy, first-responders, hospice workers and the person who bags your groceries with a smile.

I've had the privilege of helping difference-makers recover from the downward spiral that occurs when you focus your business on money. At times when they could least afford to stop thinking about money, they had the clarity to see what it was doing to their businesses and the courage to shift their focus.

Here are some examples of what I saw working with organizations whose mission was to make a difference with their products and services, but whose execution was all about money:

Manufacturing and retail organizations set a full-time focus on money. They loaded their sales teams with known "closers" and incented them for high conversion. The more they sold, the better leads they received, the more money they made and the more perks they got.

The data:

- All recognition and rewards throughout the organizations were connected to sales.
- From the customer service department to the c-suite, all personnel based their success on the size of their paychecks.
- When asked about their mission, they rarely remembered the impact-driven language of the vision and mission statements that hung framed on their walls.
- Top performing sales professionals lost momentum soon after they reached maximum commissions. They were unaware of the difference they were making as a result of their sales. They

saw customers as "prospects" and while they made their sales by building relationships, most had no interest in sustaining those relationships unless they were seeking referrals or repeat business.

- Sales managers encouraged competition over cooperation, leading to diminished teamwork, disjointed teams, pervasive back-biting, "lead stealing" and ongoing conflict.

In **organizations with in-house marketing teams**, we saw a strong push to generate campaigns that drove home value-for-the-money, money-saving discounts and fast-action sales. As they quickly discovered, these campaigns inadvertently diminished their companies' brands and led consumers to get distracted from the impact of the brands' products and services, turning all focus to price points and "deals."
The data:

- In an effort to recover from the price wars they'd created, executives passed on the pressure to all departments with instructions to cut costs, further lowering the quality and impact of their products and services.
- Purchasing departments cut costs by ordering lower quality supplies, forcing production departments to have no choice but to lower the quality of the products they produced.
- From administrative assistants to the c-suite, personnel lost respect for the products/services they represented leading to poor work ethic, poor productivity, poor teamwork, poor customer service and heated water-cooler discussions about why year-end bonuses were being cut and layoffs were coming.
- Turnover, absenteeism and conflict increased while revenues fell way below their potential.

Again, all of this happened in organizations whose missions specifically stated their primary goal was to make an impact in the lives of the people they served.

I expected this in sales organizations, but nothing prepared me for what I discovered when the restructuring of health insurance in the United States, coupled with ever-shifting economic trends, moved even the most dedicated wellness professionals to turn their focus to money.[8]

I've had the privilege of serving doctors in a wide range of specialties from neurosurgeons to primary care physicians, from cosmetic dentists to plastic surgeons, from optometrists to podiatrists and from naturopaths to chiropractors. In **private practices, hospitals and educational institutions** I watched as impact-driven men and women responded to the ever-increasing pressure to focus on money.

The data:

- Doctors who had once prided themselves on the time and care they'd always given each patient, now rushed from one to the next, averaging six minutes per patient, seeing upwards of 60 patients per day and bringing in significantly lower revenues. Where they'd once enjoyed comfortable lifestyles, now the money they brought into their practices barely covered expenses. They spent weekends and nights moonlighting at emergency rooms to make money to pay their children's college tuition. Many were forced to leave private practice to become hospital employees or partner with other doctors. Little by little, the stress they experienced separated them from the compassion that once defined their days.

- Where once there were plenty of staff to handle patient care, now nurses sat in cubicles filing insurance claims, whispering complaints about how their doctors were grumpy and counting the hours until they had to pick up their kids at childcare. Practice managers hid behind closed doors, trying desperately to keep up with ever-changing insurance codes, and listening to patient complaints about sitting in waiting rooms for hours on end.

---

8   By definition and oath, doctors are focused on impact—but when my company was hired by hundreds of private practices and hospitals to help them make more money, we saw another side of healthcare: frightened doctors, staff and patients. Frankly, it frightened me too!

- While many under-privileged people were finally able to receive healthcare that was previously out of reach, the increasing strain on understaffed hospitals and private practices added fuel to an already burning wildfire of problems for doctors, staff and patients. This led to a catastrophic increase in conflict among staff and doctors and increased stress and illness among the people who were there to help the ill.

- Where partner meetings had once been about patient review and expansion for more comprehensive patient services, now these meetings were about spreadsheet review, and typically included heated discussions about salary cuts, decreased bonuses, increased call time and lost vacations.

- As cutbacks became the norm and patients lost connections with their doctors, malpractice claims increased, causing serious problems, not only for patients and families who were maltreated, but for doctors who were wrongly accused in frivolous suits by people who sought to capitalize on difficult times. This caused insurance companies to raise malpractice premiums, adding to the strain of a system that was already in deep trouble.

- Some doctors opted out of accepting insurance so they could stop focusing on money and get back to giving patients the care they deserved. But turning away patients who couldn't pay out-of-pocket fees carried a heavy price, for the patients who lost their trusted doctors and for the doctors who had to find a way to manage the guilt (and shame) they experienced by going against their deep desires to heal everyone who needed their care.

**When difference-makers turn their
focus to money, everyone loses.**

I wish I could tell you I only found this data in organizations I was hired to study and serve, but the truth is I discovered this lesson the hard way.

By the time I was 31, I had developed and tested hundreds of sales and leadership formulas and found the unique combination that brought dramatic results in multiple industries and settings. I then used these formulas to build my first three businesses and to help local, national and international businesses grow theirs.

My results were consistently powerful, so I decided to open two more businesses—an international training and consulting company specializing in sales and leadership development and a franchise I'd purchased that enabled me to offer motivational products as follow-up to the training services I provided.

My first major contract was for a leading telecom company in the U.S. I loved this company. Not once did they ask for a referral or even for proof that I could do what I was promising. They believed I could deliver because I had launched our relationship by providing complimentary consulting that created impact for them before we ever got to the contractual stage. Most importantly, they were completely open to shifting their focus off of money and onto impact.

Our initial contract was for me to provide a training program for their external sales teams across three states and I added the franchised products to keep their momentum going post-training. To their credit, they not only accepted the additional products, they chose the option to divide their regional team into small training groups to maximize my ability to offer more individualized attention during the program.

The extended time of the contract and follow-up products increased my fees, but when I asked if that was an issue, the Director of Sales simply asked if they could pay it out over three months. That was the only conversation we ever had about money.

Each group participated in one three-day, intensive retreat where they learned formulas that were counter to any sales tactics they'd ever used. At night, we'd sit in circles and I'd help them break through personal barriers that would keep them from being comfortable using these formulas.

By the time we were done, members of each group had completely shifted their focus away from money and onto the impact they could make in people's lives as a result of installing their phone systems.

Without exception, every group reported increased sales by more than 200% in fewer than 30 days, and they continued rising for the 18 months during which we tracked their results.

It's one thing to grow your own business with your own formulas. It's a game-changer when others can use your formulas with as much—or even greater success.

The Director of Sales and Marketing couldn't say enough about the changes he saw in his team, *"Since attending your workshops, I have witnessed a transformation within my people."*

He referred me into other departments in the company and for the first time I realized I was onto something huge. From their internal sales and customer service departments to their administrative teams and managers, the results continued to be exponential and fast.

The Senior Marketing Manager shared statistics and added, *"Throughout the past we have had various sales workshops. However, none have had the high level of intensity and excellent course value that yours provided. Thanks to your superior knowledge in the sales arena, [Company] now has many of the top sales people in the industry!"*

The Associate Vice President of Customer Support wrote, *"The training that was delivered by Wendy was everything we expected and more. The response from our sales force was overwhelming and contributed to our organization's success in meeting or exceeding all of our objectives."*

The company's profits were rising and, more importantly, we saw an exponential increase in the percent of sales that were referral-based—proof positive that the formulas were doing what they'd been designed to do: enable the sales team to make an impact during each sale and to move their customers to action so they would use the phone systems and get measurable results.

Since customers were seeing measurable results, they naturally talked about their experiences with friends and word spread quickly that my client's system and service were heads-and-shoulders above the then industry leaders'.

When the vast majority of your sales are referral-based, you've mastered your Focus On Impact.

Customers were happy, employees were thriving, their leaders were ecstatic and I was more driven than ever to get my formulas into the hands of difference-making organizations worldwide.

After months on the road, I finally returned to my condo to catch up on piles of accumulated mail. I opened my bank statement and staring back at me was a balance that was so enormous, at first I thought it was a mistake.

Where did all that money come from?!

I had been so busy serving my clients, I'd completely lost track of the deposits they were sending to my account. Yet there it was—more money than I'd ever imagined I'd see in my lifetime, let alone in six months.

If I can do all of this by myself, what could I make if I had a team of people selling my services?!

Suddenly all I could think about was money. I hired a team of 10 sales professionals, took them on a 10-day retreat, trained them in my system, offered enormous salaries and placed them throughout the U.S. in lavishly decorated satellite offices.

Next, I blacked out my calendar and spent every week on the road, conducting complimentary, public workshops across the United States. I spared no expense: newspaper ads, expense accounts for my team, elaborate dinners with would-be clients, high-end venues, full-color resource guides, and gold-embossed business cards—all designed to get managers in the door, give them dinner and three hours of killer training, and then enroll them for private meetings post-event where I would personally offer consultations that brought them so much value, they'd invite me to work with their teams.

Every city yielded signed contracts adding up to millions in revenues and huge commissions for my team. They were thrilled and I was having the time of my life.

If you had enough money so you could stop thinking about money—would you work for free?

That's what I did. After giving my team their commissions, I used the deposits to cover my expenses while I gave free speeches across the country, trained non-profit volunteers, consulted for non-profit boards, spoke at schools, Rotary® meetings and women's clubs. In between, I kept offering the complimentary, promotional workshops and post-event consultations that yielded even more contracts.

I was having so much fun, I started to lose track of little things I'd always done, like sending thank-you notes and learning the names of all my attendees and taking extra care to learn about each attendee's company before a workshop.

I also stopped connecting with everyone on my team. Where in the past I'd call each team member once a day to check in, our calls became less frequent. I stopped taking them for expensive dinners to thank them and stopped flying in on surprise visits as I'd done before.

One of my team members used my low visibility as an opportunity to take advantage of the trust I'd placed in him. He accessed the account I'd opened in his town and helped himself to $100,000 in cash, using a letter forged with my signature and his employee ID. He was never found and the money was never recovered.

Among other details that I overlooked, I also stopped paying attention to what my attorneys were (and weren't) doing. As a result, I missed a huge mistake in the contracts all my new clients had signed—a critical error that left me unprotected if they cancelled or postponed their training programs.

Yet even when I noticed the omission, I didn't see any need to pay attorneys to redraft the contracts and get clients to sign again. They weren't going to cancel, at this point. Right?

Wrong. On August 2, 1990, President George H. W. Bush announced we were sending troops overseas to fight in the first Gulf War. I didn't hear the announcement because I had a firm rule about never watching the news; however I must have been the only person who hadn't heard. Suddenly our phones were ringing with cancellations and indefinite postponements.[9]

Since my contracts had no clause about cancellation/postponements, all the money we'd collected as deposits had to be sent back. That wouldn't have been a problem, except I'd already spent it all on bonuses for my team, lavish dinners for would-be clients, first class travel accommodations and huge marketing budgets.

Since this business was relatively new, I wasn't paying myself a salary and had been drawing from savings left from the sale of my first business.[10] I used whatever was left in savings to cover everything I owed my would-be clients and pay my employees' salaries. Then I started using credit cards to cover personal and business expenses. One-by-one I maxed out the cards until finally I was out of options.

I'll never forget the day I called my team members to tell them I was shutting down the satellite offices and had to let them go. It was the most difficult thing I'd ever faced in business. I'd made promises to these people and now I was turning them away. While everyone was gracious, I felt their pain deeply.

Where the sound of my phone ringing had once been cause for celebration, now the ring terrified me as creditors called morning to night to demand money I didn't have.

---

9   I later learned this was standard in times of war, where training and advertising budgets are often cut in preparation for anticipated dips in consumer spending.
10 Much of which had been lost in the Black Monday crash less than three years earlier.

**It's very hard to focus on impact when the sheriff
is hammering an eviction notice on your front door.**

I knew where I'd gone wrong and I was determined to fix it, but I didn't know how.

I'd never really understood the meaning of humiliation until I signed the bankruptcy papers. That night I cried all the tears I'd been holding in for months.

The next morning I woke up thinking about Vince Lombardi, *"Gentlemen, this is a football."*

It was time to go back to basics. For me that meant I had to stop thinking about money and Focus On Impact. It was my only way out of the hole I'd dug.

I got a full-time job selling cosmetics at a large department store. Each morning I clocked in and spent the entire day talking with customers. I never tried to sell them anything. I simply offered them complimentary information about skin care and color selection and inspired them to take time for themselves.

If they chose to buy something, I referred them on to one of the other employees, giving away commissions that would have been mine. I was still raw and afraid of being seduced by the rapid growth I knew I could create there.

The crowds of people at my counter grew with each passing day as I gave little speeches with formulas for motivating their families, co-workers and bosses, secrets to elevate self-esteem, leadership tools, communication strategies, and other topics they asked about. I rarely mentioned cosmetics, but they stayed, they listened, they bought, and the next day came back and brought their friends.

The cash registers were ringing and our counter was breaking sales records. The employees loved me because they were getting my commissions. My manager was thrilled by the amount of product our counter was moving. And me? Every night I went home feeling proud of myself for the difference I was making in people's lives. My rent and utilities were covered, and I had learned to love egg noodles and cottage cheese mixed with a touch of boysenberry jelly.

News of the dramatic increase in sales at our counter soon spread to corporate headquarters of the brand I represented and within a few months they'd hired me as a consultant. Soon after, I was back in business, conducting training programs on how to increase revenues by focusing on impact. I began each session with the story I just shared with you.

Since those days, my life has been filled with fabulous clients and abundant rewards. But to this day, I don't think about money. I leave that to my husband/business partner who carefully watches over the corporate and personal accounts.

From time to time I ask him, *"Are we doing okay?"*

He just smiles and says, *"You're doing great."* That's good enough for me.

**As long as the thank-you notes keep coming in,
I know I'm doing exactly what I need to be doing.**

It took time to completely reset my mindset and trust it to work. But now, I can't imagine running my business any other way. Of course there are times when I still think about money—planning our future, setting fees, etc., but all buying decisions in my company rest on one critical foundation:

**Will this increase my ability to make
a measurable impact on people's lives?**

If so, we go for it. If not, we don't.

You see, the secret that unlocked the vault and enabled me to bounce back from bankruptcy to produce multimillion-dollar revenues is simply this:

**Stop thinking about money and focus everything you do
on making a measurable impact on every life you touch.**

From product development, to marketing to delivery to service… turn your profit-driven business into an impact-driven business and Focus On Impact.

When You Focus On Impact, the Money Will Come.

I hope by now you see Focus On Impact isn't a "woo-woo-send-it-out-to-the-universe" thing. Focus On Impact is a strategic model that is built on a foundation of proven, tactical strategies you can use to make millions for the unique difference you bring to people's lives and enjoy every step of your journey to make it happen.

When you strategically Focus On Impact in every area of your business, not only can you make money, but you can make a LOT of money. The secret is to stop thinking about money and follow the Focus On Impact Map to make it happen.

If you've been focused on money, the first thing you've got to do is *Reset Your Mindset* to Focus On Impact. I choose the word "reset" because that's exactly what you're doing. You're not changing who you are—you're just going back to who you were before society messed with you!

Remember: impact comes naturally to you. You've been impacting lives since the day you were born! Society *taught* you to focus on money. Traditional business training *taught* you to focus on money. Business radio and TV shows *taught* you to focus on money. And you were a good student.

Just because you're good at something, doesn't mean you should do it.

Simply *Reset Your Mindset* back to where you began so you can discover the joy that comes from knowing the secure and abundant life you're enjoying is the direct result of the difference you've made in people's lives.

Sir Richard Branson is quoted as saying, *"If you aren't making a difference in other people's lives, you shouldn't be in business—it's that simple."*

How do you argue with Sir Richard Branson?

Measure your success by the number of thank you notes and referrals you receive. That's your shortest path to the money and a lifetime of fulfillment.

If you really want to reach millions, make millions and love your life along the way, it's time to develop Impact Mastery.

It all begins with Action Step # 1...

ACTION STEP #1

Notice Your Impact

There is one mistake I've seen people make over and over again. This one mistake is so huge, it can block you from achieving the success you deserve. The worst part is, most people have no idea it's happening. They know they can't move forward, but they don't know why.

The mistake is: not seeing how you impact other people.

Let's make sure you never make this mistake so you can maximize and capitalize on your impact. For the next seven days, watch how people respond to you.

- Notice how a simple smile from you impacts a stranger.
- Walk down the wrong side of a busy airport, mall, grocery aisle or sidewalk and watch how people respond.
- Notice how a heartfelt, unexpected compliment leads to a complete change in the recipient's facial coloration.
- Notice how the energy in a room shifts when you sit up straight.
- Purposefully change your rate of breathing and notice how it creates a change in how someone near you breathes.

Notice your impact. As soon as you finally see how much you impact people, then ask yourself one question:

What could I do in this world if I learned how to harness my power to impact people's lives?

The world is waiting for your impact. Start now with Action Step # 1 and then turn the page for your personal tour of the complete Focus On Impact Map!

Chapter Two

The Focus On Impact® Map

Before we had GPS, we depended on paper maps to get us from point A to point B. When I was little, my mom and I went on a lot of road trips and I was in charge of reading the special map she ordered from the AAA[11] called a TripTik®.

I loved those maps! Each one was customized based on how you wanted to experience your journey, with highlighted points determined by your unique interests and needs. The TripTik® was long and narrow, bound at the top with a spiral comb. Each page showed the next leg of your journey and while you could flip ahead to see what was coming, the map was designed so you only saw one page at a time and never got overwhelmed by how far you had left to go.

In addition to highlighting recreational stops, each page also showed road hazards, construction, probable time of travel based on

---

11   The AAA is the American Automobile Association, a non-profit organization that is still very popular across the United States. And yes, you can still get a TripTik® there!

17

predicted traffic patterns and detours that would otherwise have gotten you totally lost.

**Never begin an important journey without an expert
to guide you—or at the very least, a proven map.**

Our last big road trip was when she took me to visit college campuses. I wasn't sure I wanted to go to college and I remember looking out at the passing scenery, completely confused about where my life was headed.

"Wouldn't it be great if we had a TripTik® for our lives?" I asked.

"I AM your TripTik®" she smiled back.

And she was.

So now, permit me to be your TripTik® as we take a quick tour of your Focus On Impact Map so you see the complete journey that lies ahead. Then, we'll *customize* your map, one city at a time, so you can see precisely what it takes to capitalize on your uniqueness so you can build the business and life that's ideal for you.

Your Map

There are 10 cities on your Focus On Impact Map and the secret is to **follow the map in sequence**, visiting each city in order until you reach your chosen destination.[12]

CITY # 1: DEFINE

The first stop is a magical city where you'll find the clarity you need to determine precisely what you want your unique impact to be, what you want to get as a result of your impact and how you'll make it happen without sabotaging your own success.[13] By the time you leave DEFINE, you'll know where you're going, what it will take to get there and which road blocks you'll need to remove so you can quickly and easily get where you want to be!

---

12 For your downloadable, color copy of the Focus On Impact Map, visit www.
    FocusOnImpact.com/resources

13 Far too many difference-makers skip this critical step, wasting precious time (and
    money).

CITY # 2: DISCOVER

There is no doubt in my mind your unique impact is a missing piece this world needs. The secret is to identify your uniqueness so you can access and infuse it into every area of your business. In the city of DISCOVER, you'll use a scientific formula to find the unique gift only you can bring to this crowded global market so you can differentiate your brand, create one-of-a-kind products and services and make the difference you were born to bring to people's lives.

CITY # 3: DETERMINE

Traditional business advice urges you to narrow your niche. While this is an effective marketing strategy in traditional businesses, it causes a serious problem for difference-makers. When the goal is to make an impact, narrowing your niche is unfair to all the people who could be served by your products and services. It's also unfair to you! So in the City of DETERMINE, you'll learn how to widen your niche and serve the market that's best for you. Hint: Your market will likely include people you never would have considered!

CITY # 4: DESIGN

Most entrepreneurs have a crystal clear vision of the lifestyle they'd like to live *after* they've made their first million. The problem is they burn out along the way and never make it happen. As a difference-maker, it's critically important you never burn out because the world needs you to make this work. So in the City of DESIGN, I'll show you how to design your lifestyle so you can live the life you want *while* you grow your business so you can love your life now and all along your journey.

CITY # 5: DEVELOP

Once you've been through the first four cities, you'll have everything you need to DEVELOP one-of-a-kind products and services that will produce a measurable impact. There is a proven formula for developing your ideal retail and service mix so people will love to buy, use and share everything you create! You'll get this plug-n-play formula in the City of DEVELOP.

CITY # 6: DIFFERENTIATE

In today's global market, you can impact millions (even billions) of people with one click as long as you know how to get people to find you, follow you and send all their friends to your door. The key is to make sure you're serving up practical impact on multiple platforms so people can easily grab your impact and associate your unique difference with their unique lives. In this city you'll learn how to DIFFERENTIATE your impact through impact-driven content marketing that sets you up as the expert in your industry and differentiates your products and services as the ideal solution for them without sleazy selling or tactics that leave you wanting to take a shower! Get ready for classy, powerful and impactful marketing fun!

CITY # 7: DELIVER

Regardless of how amazing your products and services are, the simple fact is they're useless if people don't buy and use what you've got! To make that happen, you've got to know how to ethically move people to action so they click, like, share, buy and use your products and services. In the City of DELIVER, you'll discover the Science of Impact™ and get concrete formulas to yield measurable results!

CITY # 8: DECIDE

The more success you build, the more people will surface with advice to grow your business further. But how do you DECIDE which advice is best for you and your business? In this city, you'll learn how to choose the right mentors, find your strongest solutions quickly, manage conflicting advice and pull the best from all that's available to you to make sure it's a direct fit for your impact.

CITY # 9: DIVERSIFY

The greatest growth you'll ever experience will come the day you enter the City of DIVERSIFY so you can capitalize on all you have to offer through the power of impact-driven collaboration. The world is filled with difference-makers and in this city, you'll get my proven formulas to choose collaborative partners, create huge results through collaborative projects, develop promotional opportunities through strategic partnerships and enjoy the support of people who really get you. You'll never be alone in the City of DIVERSIFY.

CITY # 10: DARE

Whether you're a solopreneur or CEO of an empire, all difference-makers reach a point after they build their impact when they're not sure where to go next. In this step you'll discover the hidden power of the Focus On Impact Map so you can keep your impact growing strong in a way that's right for you. In the City of DARE you'll find your solution to go bigger with your impact and always love your life!

And there you have it, your Focus On Impact Map, the *only* step-by-step strategic process ever created, tested and proven effective for difference-makers. This Map has been used by a wide variety of men and women around the globe to maximize and capitalize on their impact—and now it's your turn! Get motivated with Action Step # 2 and then we'll visit the City of DEFINE!

ACTION STEP #2

Measure Your Impact

For the next seven days, every time you brush your teeth, look in the mirror and ask yourself this question:

Are you making the impact you want to be making?

I've asked myself that question twice a day since 1983. I'm inviting you to do this for only one week, but I will tell you, the more you ask this question, the more your eyes will open to a vast world of opportunities that await you when you Focus On Impact.

The world is waiting for your impact. Turn the page for City # 1 on your Focus On Impact Map!

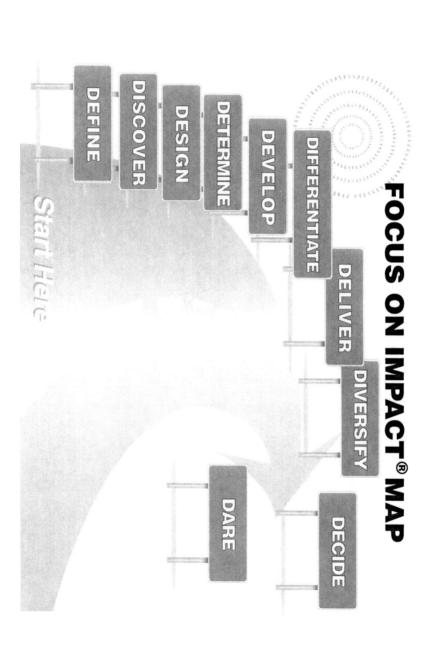

FOCUS ON IMPACT® MAP

Start Here

- DEFINE
- DISCOVER
- DESIGN
- DETERMINE
- DEVELOP
- DIFFERENTIATE
- DELIVER
- DIVERSIFY
- DARE
- DECIDE

Chapter Three

DEFINE YOUR IMPACT ACTION FORMULA

If you woke up tomorrow morning and magically found you had everything you truly want, how would your life be different?

've asked this question of well-over one million men and women around the globe—in speaking engagements, media interviews, coaching calls, executive retreats, private workshops, and in all my bestselling books.

Why do I keep asking the same question? Because the sad truth is most difference-makers have no idea how to answer it, let alone how to turn their dreams into reality. It's been estimated that 8 out of 10 entrepreneurs fail[14] and my research shows the failure rate to be even higher among impact-driven entrepreneurs.

So why do so many difference-makers fail? Common wisdom blames under-capitalization, but in my experience lack of clarity is the biggest culprit. Capital is useless to you until you know what to do with

---

14   Forbes.com

it. That begins by defining the what, where, how, who, when and why of your impact.

Even if you're an employee in a multi-national corporation, the owner of a franchise, or a member of an MLM team, your success journey will be different than any one else under your brand umbrella. Why? Because you're unique.

Your Map must be customized to your unique dreams, barriers, gifts, perspectives, personality, products, services, market and lifestyle.

Life is far too short to settle for less than you truly want—in your business or your life. But how do you *get* what you want? And what is the shortest distance between where you are and where you want to be?

It all begins by getting complete clarity on your impact and defining your formula to make it happen.

STEP 1: DEFINE YOUR IMPACT

What is the IMPACT you want to make and what do you want your IMPACT to get for you?

One of my favorite parts of my live events happens during each break when I connect with attendees one-to-one.

"What brings you here?" I ask.

"I want to make an impact!"

"Great!" I respond. *"What impact do you want to make?"*

What comes next is as varied as my attendees, but you'll notice a common thread,

"I want to make people happy,"

"I want to be a speaker,"

"I want to get my products into every home."

"I want to become a bestselling author."

"I want to grow a multi-million dollar business."

All very exciting goals, but none of these responses address my question. Defining your impact isn't about what *you* want to do.

Defining your impact is about clarifying what you want *others* to do, be and have *after* they have consumed your message, product or service.

If you focus on the aftereffect of your impact, then you will be able to make it happen by reverse-engineering the result. The secret is to define your impact so it's measurable.

Imagine it's six months from now and you've made your impact on 10,000 people. Now imagine you're in a hot air balloon floating above the people you've served. Look at them carefully. What specifically are they doing (or not doing) that is different than what they were doing *before* they experienced your message, product or service? How has that difference impacted *other* areas of their lives?

Remember: your initial impact is like the pebble you toss into a pond. Your pebble (impact) will create a series of ripples (results) that get sequentially bigger and further away from the initial source (you). So what is your initial pebble and what are your ripples?

Each impact creates results that lead to other results, ultimately affecting areas of people's lives you may never see. This is your ultimate impact. You may never see it personally, but you'll hear about it in *thank you* notes and social posts like, *"I bought your X and loved it," "I expected to get Y but the best part was it also brought me Z,"* and *"Everyone is asking me how this happened and I'm telling them all about your X—Thank you!"*

Your ultimate impact will be the RESULT of every ripple of impact that comes before it.

Now is the time to get crystal clarity on the measurable outcomes you want to make happen for people and then focus on creating one ripple at a time. Your initial impact will form the foundation for everything that comes next.

Once you've defined all your impact ripples, you'll be ready to define everything you need so you'll be *able* and *willing* to develop, market, deliver and capitalize on your impact.

That begins with Step 2…

STEP 2: DEFINE YOUR ACTION FORMULA™

I've been actively studying business development since 1974 and there is one thing all successful businesses have in common:

If you know the best actions to take and you're willing and able to take those actions, you're likely to succeed!

This book is showing you the best actions to maximize and capitalize on your unique impact, but it's up to you to take those actions! To help make sure you move yourself to action, use my internationally-acclaimed, Action Formula[15]…

Desire + Resources + Permission = ACTION!

Let's go through each component of the formula so you can use it to grow your impact.

DESIRE

DESIRE is everything you want and what all of that will get for you. Simple enough, yet it's one of the most misunderstood components of success. In fact, of the 100,000+ people I've personally queried, 100% discovered details of their DESIRES they'd never seen before.

The more you know about your DESIRE, the more power you'll have to keep going at those moments when your journey gets hard.

To define your DESIRE, answer these four questions:

Question 1. If you woke up tomorrow morning and magically found you were already making a measurable impact on the lives of everyone you want to reach with your message, products and/or services, how would your life be different?

---

15   To read the entertaining story of how four characters use the Action Formula to get everything they want (in business and life), read *Shatter Your Speed Limits*®.

✓ What would you be doing that you don't do now?

✓ What could you *stop* doing that you have to do now?

✓ What would you own that you don't have now?

✓ What would you be feeling that you don't get to feel enough of now?

✓ What could you stop feeling that you feel way too often now?

✓ What would you get to be that you've always wanted to be?

✓ What could you stop being that you've felt you had to be?

Question 2. If everything you described above were happening right now, what would that get for you?

Question 3. And what would *that* get for *you*?[16]

Question 4. Rate yourself on a scale of 1 to 10, where 1 = *I guess that would be nice* and 10 = *I want this so badly I can feel it burning in my soul!*

If you're not a "10" then add more specifics to your answers to questions 1, 2 and 3 until your list becomes a

---

16 I created an *Impact Action Formula Planning Packet* for you so you can write out your answers to all the questions in this chapter. Download yours at FocusOnImpact.com/resources

Aviva Goldfarb had a clear vision of the impact she wanted to make in the world: She wanted families to enjoy healthy dinners together on a regular basis without experiencing the stress involved in making it happen. The problem: in today's world, families are busy! Who has time to plan, shop and cook—let alone sit down together at a table?

Aviva was a solid "10." Driven to make her impact in her own family and in families around the globe, she created an easy-to-use, meal-planning tool that adapts to each individual family's needs and tastes. She placed this powerful tool in an online community where parents get weekly shopping lists, menus, recipes and more. The end result? At the time of this printing, more than 60,000 families have been served by Aviva's impact through her online portal—and that doesn't include the millions who have been exposed to her impact through major media appearances and her books. This is what happens when you Focus On Impact and clearly define a measurable impact.

solid "10." You see, the more difficult the goal, the more difficult it will be to make it happen and the more motivation you'll need to make it happen. So what's missing on your list that would make you a "10"?

Once you understand what you'll get as a result of making your impact, the next question is: *What do you need so* you'll be *able to make it happen?* And for that you need component # 2 of the Action Formula.

RESOURCES

Every entrepreneur wants his/her business to succeed, but if wanting it were enough, there would be no failures.

Regardless of your clarity regarding what you want and how deeply driven you are to achieve it, you have to be ABLE to capture your dreams.

For that you need easy access to the necessary RESOURCES to build your business, for example:

✓ A customized, sequential strategic plan to build your impact-driven business[17]
✓ A list of ACTIONS you need to take to maximize each step of your strategic plan[18]
✓ A concrete plan to generate, manage and use the money you need to operate your business and support you as you grow
✓ Education, experience and skills to design your strategy and implement it
✓ A team to support you (virtual assistants, employees, contract labor, trusted mentors, vendors, friends and family)[19]
✓ A prioritized schedule to assure you use your time effectively[20]
✓ Tangible assets for day-to-day operations (a usable work environment, office supplies, equipment, transportation, communication tools, website, software, hardware)

---

17 This book provides your step-by-step, sequential strategic plan to build an impact-driven business and strategies to customize it to fit for you.
18 The Action Steps at the end of each chapter will guide you and if you have any questions, simply visit our community at Facebook.com/focusonimpact
19 See Chapter 11 on how to decide which advice is best for you
20 See Chapter 5 on how to design your ideal impact lifestyle

✓ Collaborative partners to support and promote your impact[21]
✓ Physical energy (health) to do what it takes

It's critically important that you define your RESOURCES in advance by making three lists: (1) what you need to make this happen, (2) what assets you've got that you can use and (3) what is missing that you need. Then, for each item that's missing, answer the following questions:

1. What actions will you take to get this?
2. Who will you get to help you?
3. By what date will you have it?

The more detailed your lists, the more likely you'll be to collect all the RESOURCES you need![22]

Knowing which RESOURCES you need and gathering them together is a critical step to building your impact-driven business. Yet even after you collect all your RESOURCES, there's no guarantee you'll take all of the actions you've outlined. Remember, there are three components of the Action Formula. So let's look at the most overlooked component of success…

PERMISSION

Okay, you've defined the impact you want to make and what that will get for you. You've defined all the ACTIONS you need to take so you can get what you want, and gathered together all the RESOURCES you need so you're ABLE to take action… is that enough?

No. If wanting something and being able to get it were enough, there would be a lot more success in every area of life, from weight loss to financial freedom.

There is a universal truth in business (and life): *people sabotage their own success.*

---

21 See Chapter 10 on how to create impact-driven collaborative partnerships
22 Download your Impact Action Formula Planning Packet at FocusOnImpact.com/resources.

If you're smiling right now, you know exactly what I mean.

In my initial call with every client, one of my first questions is, *"What is your #1 success barrier?"* The clients who end up building the greatest successes are those who initially responded by saying, *"My greatest barrier is ME!"*

> **We have to be WILLING to take the necessary actions to make our impact and to live with the consequences of our actions (success or failure).**

Oh I'm totally willing! Just tell me what to do and I'll do it!

Really? If I told you the action you need to take to achieve success is leave your family and never see or speak to them again, would you do it?

Ummm.

Right. You hesitate. So the two questions to ask yourself are, (1) *What is the downside of achieving the success you envision?* and (2) *What will you do to accommodate that?*

In other words, it's one thing to want to reach millions, make millions and love your life along the way, but are you ready for the changes your success will bring to your life?

What will I do if this actually works?!

No matter how fabulous your vision of impact is, there is probably some part of you that has a valid reason for not wanting it to happen. It's important to get that out of the darkness where you can see it and address it. Because when everything starts rolling, you're going to need every part of you on board and ready to go!

Is that all there is to PERMISSION? Ah, if only it were that easy. There may be other roadblocks on your Journey of Impact.

Cultural and Personal Rules

Difference-makers are rule-breakers, yet we get very uncomfortable around breaking rules that are important to us. Some of our rules are around the ethics we hold about business, so one of the most important things you can do in the City of DEFINE is to get clarity on your ethical pillars.

It isn't my place to tell you what your ethical pillars should be, but I encourage you to define your ethics so you'll know where your PERMISSIONS will take you—and where they won't.

PERMISSION barriers also pop up when we come face-to-face with situations and people that go against rules we carry deep inside about what's okay to do and not do, be and not be and have and not have.

Rules are taught to us (verbally and non-verbally) early in life and stay with us as we move through our lives. We learn rules from family, teachers, clergy, neighbors, friends, bosses, media, and by the culture we're exposed to every day.

For example, try walking down the left side of a crowded airport walkway in the U.S. and watch the glaring faces of passersby. You're breaking a rule and everyone scorns you for your behavior. Yet, the same action in the U.K. would go unnoticed as everyone there is doing the same thing!

Some of the most powerful rules we follow today were given to us long before we were old enough to know we were learning them! We watched the behaviors of those around us, we learned from their responses to our behaviors, and for the rest of our lives, we followed their rules...

Work hard... Be perfect... Don't ask for help... Be a good employee... Don't rock the boat... Keep your eye on your money... Never talk to strangers... Don't trust anyone... Keep your thoughts to yourself... Don't air dirty laundry... Don't make mistakes... Don't break family traditions... Moms shouldn't work... Dads must work... Be happy with what you've got... Don't stick up for yourself... Don't break the rules...

And the list goes on and on. Society expects you to follow the rules. The question is, are any of the rules you learned growing up blocking your PERMISSION to succeed?

Rules take away our freedom to choose.

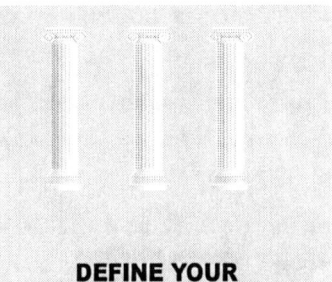

DEFINE YOUR ETHICAL PILLARS

Choose three Ethical Pillars upon which your impact-driven business will sit. Once you define those, you'll have complete clarity on the rules you will not permit to be broken—by you or anyone else! For example, here are the 3 ethical pillars of my company, Professional Impact, Inc.

- **Fairness**—If something isn't fair to one or more people involved, we won't do it.

- **Respect**—We focus on helping our clients get what *they* want, without imposing our opinions about what they *should* want and by honestly informing them regarding whether we are able and willing to help them make it happen.

- **Impact** — Our mission is to make a measurable impact on

For example, a common rule taught to children is, *be strong*. This rule is typically passed on when it's deemed inappropriate to feel or show emotions or give in to pain. Are there circumstances in life where that rule would help you make your impact? Absolutely. Imagine you're invited to present at the United States Senate and that morning you're hit with a stomach virus. Do you give in to your desire to curl up under the covers or do you tough it out and show up? You'd probably do what I did—be strong!

But what if you're speaking to an audience of 15,000 people about something you feel passionate about? And what if you want them to feel the passion too? To make your impact, you've got to give yourself PERMISSION to break your rule and express the full spectrum of your passion. As tears roll down your face, your audience will be crying right along with you and your impact will be profound! But that's not going to happen if you follow your rule. You'll have to be strong no matter what and your impact will be muted.

Guiding Rules

Sometimes the rules that block success are those we create ourselves. Everyone experiences stressful situations in life and when the stress goes beyond tolerable limits, we create rules to assure we'll never have to experience that discomfort again.

Let's say you're eight years old and your best friend makes a promise to meet you after school. You wait for him but he never shows up. Finally, the school buses leave and you're left all alone with no way to get home. You call your mom to pick you up and she punishes you by taking away your video games for a week. Sitting in your room, mad and embarrassed, you make a new rule so you'll never be in this situation again, *"I can't trust anyone!"* That makes perfect sense when you're a kid. But 30 years later, when your new business partner is five minutes late for a meeting, you suddenly find yourself thinking, *"I knew I shouldn't trust this guy!"* One year later, you wonder why the business never took off.

people's lives so they, in turn, can make an impact on every life they touch. We only accept invitations for service where we see an opportunity to achieve our mission.

What are your ethical pillars? Define them now and your impact will be supported by a powerful foundation.

Self-made rules become *Guiding Rules* and are often the single greatest cause of personal and professional failure. Guiding Rules dictate many of the choices we make in our lives and we bring those rules right into business. The solution is to discover your Guiding Rule(s) and break through them permanently so you'll be free to make all business decisions from a place of clarity that isn't being colored by events that happened years ago.

Every entrepreneur has at least one hidden barrier that keeps him/her from taking actions that would lead to success.

Below is a list of the most common Guiding Rules we've seen among impact-driven men and women.[23] As you read each one, you may experience a sense of familiarity or even feel a slight jolt go through your body. If so, it's likely these are words you've heard inside your own head more than once in your life.

---

23 In private practice and in training programs.

I'm not good enough... I'm not worthy... I'm not smart enough... There must be something wrong with me... I'm on my own... I'll show you ... There's nothing I can do about it... I have to get this done even if it kills me... I don't need anyone... I'll keep my mouth shut... I won't ask for help... I won't get close so I don't get hurt... I don't matter... I'll sleep when I'm dead...

Of all the actions you'll take to bring your impact to the world, perhaps the most important action of your life will be your decision to identify your personal PERMISSION barriers and break through them.[24]

So there you have it, the formula to move yourself to action so you'll implement everything I'm bringing you in this book:

D + R + P = ACTION!

The Action Formula is a mathematical equation, so the more difficult the action, the more DESIRE, RESOURCES and PERMISSION you'll need.

When you define your Impact Action Formula, there is absolutely nothing that will stop you! Take time now to do Action Step #3 so you'll be ready to move forward to the City of DISCOVER!

---

24 If you'd like help to identify and break through your PERMISSION barriers, visit FocusOnImpact.com/resources to meet my go-to resource for our clients, Dr. Hal Dibner.

ACTION STEP #3

Define Your Impact Action Formula

It's time to define your unique Impact Action Formula! To help you make it happen, I've created a special gift for you.

Go to www.FocusOnImpact.com/resources to download your personal **Impact Action Formula Planning Packet** – one for you and one for each member of your team. Print out the entire packet and put it somewhere you'll be every day where you can take about five minutes to add to your lists.

Your Planning Packet will take you through the entire process of defining your Impact Action Formula, with questions that will help you identify precisely what you want, what you've got and what you'll need to make it happen. It will also help you find barriers that could keep you from letting yourself have everything you truly want.

Your unique IMPACT, DESIRES, RESOURCES and PERMISSIONS will determine how you customize the Focus On Impact Map to build your success!

Even if you're already enjoying a successful business, I invite you to define your Impact Action Formula – you may discover the missing piece you need to take your impact further![25]

The world is waiting for your impact. Turn the page to visit City # 2 on your Focus On Impact Map!

---

25 The larger your team, the more powerful this becomes. Engage your employees by inviting them to define their individual Impact Action Formulas. Then encourage each department to collaboratively develop their departmental Impact Action Formula. Finally, bring together your executive team to collaboratively define your company Impact Action Formula.

Chapter Four

DISCOVER YOUR UNIQUE GIFT

***Each of us is born with a unique gift—something we
do naturally that no one in the world can match.***

*I know there's something different about me, my company, my products
and services and how I help people...it's just hard to explain.*

Sound familiar? If so, please know you're not alone. I've yet to meet
an entrepreneur who can clearly explain how s/he is different from
everyone else in a way that helps us really get it. That's probably why we
hear so many cynics say,

"There's nothing new under the sun."

Nevertheless, each time a child is born, something new appears
under the sun. How we then nurture that child's uniqueness determines
what comes next.

The future of our planet depends on innovation and that means we
desperately need you to identify what you can bring to us that's new,

fresh, untried and out-of-the-box. This is great news for you because once you figure it out, people will rush to get it!

To make that happen, you've first got to discover your *unique gift*.

WHAT IS A UNIQUE GIFT?

Every day you do things you take for granted, from walking across the room to sending a text. But there is also something you do that makes others look at you with total awe.

"How do you DO that?!"

"Do what?" you reply innocently.

"That thing you do! It's amazing! I wish I could do that!"

You don't think it's particularly amazing—you do it all the time—but others are deeply impressed.

Or maybe that's never happened to you. Like so many people, maybe you've never noticed your special gift. If so, I can tell you with absolute certainty, there's something VERY special about you. And people have seen it. They just haven't told you.

When I was studying to become a psychotherapist, one of my favorite mentors was Dr. Erving Polster, author of *Every Person's Life is Worth a Novel*. One day, I asked Dr. Polster if he ever got bored just listening to people's problems all day long. What he said forever changed my perspective on people and guides me to this day.

"Wendy," he said, *"Everyone you'll ever meet in your entire life will have something about him or her that will fascinate you. Your job is to find that one thing."*

Ever since that day, I've spent my life looking for the one thing that fascinates me about everyone I meet—and I always find it!! The longer I get to talk with people, the more I see additional things that fascinate me until finally I'm able to put it all together to show them their unique gift—something they've never noticed about how they think or behave that's truly special. I ask about it and without exception, it turns out they readily recognize that this "thing" has been part of their lives as far back as they can remember.

This has been an invaluable tool in my coaching because once you know your unique gift, you can quickly extrapolate how that will play into everything you do to bring your impact to the world. That one piece of information sets off a chain reaction generating ideas that are truly different and yielding one-of-a-kind products and services and distinctive branding that helps them stand apart in a world of faceless competitors.

I'd been helping clients find their unique gifts for many years when one day, I was conducting a small workshop called, *"Your Unique Gift."* One of the attendees said, *"Wendy, your unique gift is that you always find our unique gifts! It's magic!"*

"Thanks, but it's not magic," I said, *"I'm just outside your forest so it's easy for me to see."*

"But none of US ever see it in each other. And you DO!" someone added.

As soon as he said that, I wanted to figure out how I do it so I could teach people to find their own gifts.[26] As it turned out, it's not magic at all; it's science.

THE SCIENCE OF UNIQUENESS

I process ideas best when I talk them through, so I asked my husband to come talk with me while I was swimming.[27] He sat on the deck under an umbrella while I bicycled through the water and talked him through the labyrinth of my own unique gift.

"You've known me longer than anyone," I began. *"So what do you think is my unique gift?"*

---

26 That's what happens when you Focus On Impact. By teaching you how I go about finding someone's unique gift, you can then use that information to help more people than I will ever reach. And that makes my impact exponential. Cool stuff, yes?

27 Hal and I have known each other since 1985. He's been with me for many of my greatest triumphs and held me through some of my worst nightmares. There's no one else in the world who knows me the way he does! Who do you have in your life who knows you inside and out?

Without hesitation he said,

"You're an elegant puzzle-solver. You always come up with the one brilliant idea that no one has ever thought of or you find the one thing they need to do to succeed or the one piece that pulls an entire system together or the one missing strategy that changes their sales and as soon as you say it, everyone just nods their heads and says, 'Yep—that's it!' And you do it <u>every single time</u>. It's (bleep)ing amazing!"

As soon as he said it I realized that was exactly what I'd done my entire life. But I'd never thought it was all that cool. It's just what I'd always done.

Hal and I talked so long my fingers shriveled, but I didn't want to get out of the pool for fear we'd lose our momentum. We discussed that my "gift" of solving intricate puzzles ran in my family. They were all puzzle-solvers in their own ways, but I'd never made the connection until that day in the pool. By the time we were done, we'd traced the path of my unique gift back to my grandfather. I was infused with puzzle-power. [28]

So why couldn't I solve my own puzzle? Because I was in the middle of it.

It's absolutely impossible to find your own unique gift— but you can help others find it for you!

While we'd identified my unique gift had its foundation in my family, there had to be more to it than just DNA or else everyone in my family would have used their puzzle-solving "gifts" in the same way.

---

28 My grandfather pioneered the development of pensions and other employee benefit plans in the United States. Hundreds of millions of employees today enjoy coverage under plans that were designed by him. My mother had an extraordinary talent for calculating probabilities (she discovered a system to accurately predict winners of football games that was infallible—and she did it just for fun!). She was also obsessed with crossword puzzles. When I was a kid my mom and her sister would sit on the phone and do the *New York Times* Sunday Crossword Puzzle (in pen). My aunt was editor of *Bridge World Magazine* for many years until she became a psychotherapist. Her bedroom was filled to the ceiling with jigsaw puzzles. And that's just on my mother's side.

After much analysis, I outlined the 7 Factors that contribute to the formation of our unique gifts. I'll share them with you here and then I'll reveal for you the simplest path to finding your own unique gift.[29]

THE 7 FACTORS OF YOUR UNIQUE GIFT

Factor # 1: DNA

Deep inside your DNA is the unique combination of all the gifts that were passed on to you via your maternal and paternal ancestors,[30] Look at their occupations, education, how they decorated their homes, any little things that stand out for you. What patterns do you see?

What amazes you about the patterns you see? What you see is part of your unique gift!

Factor # 2: Brain Wiring

Neuropsychologists have long agreed our unique brain wiring determines much of how we respond to our world. There are tests you can take to determine your "personality type,"[31] but the bottom line is your unique brain dictates some of the ways you respond to your world, the choices you make in your daily life, the behaviors you exhibit and so much more. All of that is a key factor in the formation of your unique gift. As you look at your daily behaviors, what patterns do you see?

What amazes you about the patterns you see?

Factor # 3: Likes/Dislikes

Most people never take the time to notice why they like what they like (or why they don't like what they don't like). We make choices all day

---

29 To download your own Unique Gift Discovery Sheet, go to FocusOnImpact.com/resources

30 If you were adopted and don't have access to your family tree, or if your family history brings up memories you'd rather avoid, skip DNA and move on to Factor # 2. There are plenty of signposts ahead to help you find your unique gift!

31 There are many tests available such as Myers-Briggs MBTI® and DISC®, but the most important piece of this is how your brain leads you to choose certain ACTIONS in your life. See Chapter 5 for the system I created called Action Types™.

long, yet we never stop to figure out what specifically makes us watch one TV show over another or what makes us choose to be alone one moment and want to be with people the next.

People will tell you they *naturally gravitate* towards the activities and people they like. That's very true—and a huge part of your unique gift! Now I'm inviting you to become consciously aware of what you like and dislike so you can see an important aspect of your uniqueness.

Watch for your patterns of likes and dislikes. What amazes you about the patterns you see?

Factor # 4: Instinctive Response

One of the most powerful reflections of your unique gift will appear when you become aware of what you've always done *naturally*. When you were little, how did you entertain yourself when you were bored? What were the things you did that brought applause from your family? What was your *secret power*? Today when friends ask for your help or advice, what do you automatically do first, and how do you typically help them?

Identify patterns in the behaviors that have come naturally to you all your life—without conscious forethought. What amazes you about the patterns you see?

Factor # 5: Social Influences

You could have been born with an extraordinary gift for music, but if you were raised on a deserted island, having never been exposed to any music, the likelihood of you ever fostering your gift for music by making music would be next to none. Nevertheless, you would find a way to use your gift in some other way.

> **Your gift is your gift—nothing changes that. How you choose to use your gift is the changeable factor.**

We're exposed to so many social influences throughout our lives, and it all comes together to influence our choices in what we do, how we think and what we feel—environment, culture, family, teachers, clergy, media, books, art, television, peers…the list is endless. All of these come together to influence us in so many ways and that has a huge impact on how we nurture and develop our unique gifts.

What are the patterns you see when you look back over the influences you've had in your life? How have they affected you—particularly with respect to making life choices? What amazes you about your pattern of influences?

Factor # 6: Education and Skills

Likes and dislikes, combined with DNA, brain wiring and social influences, all come together to impact what turns us on (and off) throughout our educational process. It determines which courses we sail through and which ones cause us endless nights of struggle.

The education we receive, the skills we develop, the things we master with no effort at all…all of this is a function of—and a clue about—our unique gift.

Think back on your education and the skills you've developed as a result. Do you see a pattern in the classes you enjoyed, the skills you've developed, the things you learned and never used? What amazes you about the pattern you see?

Factor # 7: Life and Work Experiences

Life and work experiences can be placed into two categories: things that happen to us, and things we make happen as a result.

Look back over the experiences you've had throughout your life—the jobs you've worked, the relationships that were important to you, the vacations you've loved and the moments you could have happily lived without…the more you run the movie of your life through your mind, the more you'll start to see recurring patterns.

What patterns do you see? What amazes you about the pattern of your experiences?

REVIEW ALL YOUR ACTION PATTERNS

When we stop and really look at the 7 Factors of our unique gifts, we begin to see a recurring theme—a pattern that keeps repeating itself over and over and over again. The challenge is, it's virtually impossible to identify our own patterns. That's why I brought all those people into the workshop to help them.

One after another shared the information I requested about these 7 Factors and, without exception, I identified each of their unique gifts and then held them as they cried with relief and joy over finally seeing the unique gift they were given. Some of the comments they shared,

"I always knew there was something different about me; I just didn't know what it was."

"THAT'S what I've been doing all my life! I just never had words for it!"

"How do you do that?! You just pick it out of thin air, and it's dead on target!"

"Now I know how to tell people what I do that's different! It's about time, considering I've been doing this for 25 years!"

"Wow! The marketing copy just writes itself! SO cool!"

While everyone was celebrating, I was secretly miserable. I'd thought I was going to teach them how to find their own unique gifts, and yet I had to be the one to tell them what I saw. Even they said they couldn't have found their gifts without me.

Regardless of my attendees' endorsements of the workshop, it was several weeks before I got past my sadness about what seemed like such a failure. Then one day I realized I'd made a huge mistake! The reason I had to ask them all the questions about their 7 Factors was because I didn't know them well enough to just *"pick it out of thin air."* Yet, when I'd asked my husband to identify my gift, he was able to do it in the blink of an eye.

I launched a mini research project at my next speaking engagement. I was the keynote speaker at a multi-day conference, and as part of my speech I gave everyone in the room an assignment. They were to call home and ask one question and then come find me during the rest of the week to give me the answer.

Lo and behold, everyone who did the assignment reported they had, in fact, identified their unique gift, that it had been a total surprise and, at the same time, they absolutely knew it was accurate. I was so excited I tried it again at my next speaking engagement and got the same response. Since then, I've used this method over and over with uncanny accuracy.

Want to know what it is? Just do your Action Step below and then as we continue creating your Focus On Impact Map you'll know precisely how to use your unique gift to make your unique impact in the world through one-of-a-kind products and services and effective marketing! For now, just remember this:

You've been using your gift all your life, although in all likelihood you were completely unaware of its existence or impact on others. Imagine all you could accomplish if you used your unique gift on purpose! Let's make it happen with Action Step # 4...and then I'll help you make sure you love your life all along the way of building and growing your business as we visit the City of DESIGN!

ACTION STEP #4

Discover Your Unique Gift!

Find people who have known you for more than one year and ask them this question:

"What have you seen me do that you think is amazing?"

If they can't answer you immediately, feed them the patterns you discovered going through your 7 Factors above.

Keep asking people - the more the better. Then, make a list of all the answers you received and look for the pattern – that's your unique gift!

If you're working with a team, invite every member of your team to discover their unique gifts so you can maximize their effectiveness and capitalize on everything they bring to your company.

If you have trouble interpreting your pattern, come to our Facebook Community Page at Facebook.com/focusonimpact and ask for input. Together we'll find the gift you were born to bring our world! And once you know it, you'll be ready to make it happen!

The world is waiting for your impact. Turn the page for City # 3 of your Focus On Impact Map!

Chapter Five

DESIGN
YOUR IDEAL
LIFESTYLE

Someday I want to...

The fantasy: *you're lying on a hammock under a palm tree, peacefully rocking back and forth in the warm breeze while money is automatically deposited into your bank account.*

The reality: you're up at 2:00 a.m. making lists, posting on social, organizing your calendar, trying to figure out how to use software someone suggested you buy and cursing quietly so you won't wake sleeping family members—all the while counting the diminishing hours you'll have to sleep before you'll have to get moving for real-life responsibilities (work, children, appointments, etc.).

Yes, difference-makers are amazing plate spinners. The question is:

Are you living the life you want—or the life you've got?

It's time to stop dreaming of the lifestyle you want while you live a crazy existence to make it happen. That's precisely why so many difference-makers burn out before they have the chance to make their greatest impact.

There is a better way. In the City of DESIGN, you're going to design your ideal lifestyle so you can live it now *while* you're building your impact!

Your business should be built around the life you want to live—not the other way around!

It begins by deciding HOW you want to live. Then in Chapters 7, 8, and 9 you'll choose how you're going to develop, differentiate and deliver your impact so it fits into your ideal lifestyle. This is how you'll love your life all the way to the top!

It begins right now by discovering how you can capitalize on your unique brain!

YOUR ACTION TYPE

You were born pre-wired for an ideal working lifestyle and now we're going to capitalize on that so you can do what comes naturally to you instead of having to constantly conform to a lifestyle that isn't right for you.

Look at the chart on Page 50. There you'll find four distinct Action Types representing a combination of characteristics. As you look at the chart, you'll likely find that you fit into more than one category. That's normal.

Place a check next to every characteristic that fits you at different times in your daily life. Next, circle the Action Type that *best* describes you when you're most happy. Then, identify the Action Type that is you when you're most stressed.

When you design your working lifestyle, choose activities that will let you capitalize on your Happy and Stressed Action Types. This will enable you to spend the majority of your life in your comfort zone so you'll more easily engage in the actions you select to grow your

ACTION TYPES

	Connector	Enthusiast	Thinker	Commander
Your Appearance Tends to be	▪ Casual ▪ Conforming	▪ Fashionable ▪ Stylish	▪ Formal ▪ Conservative	▪ Businesslike ▪ Functional
Your Most Comfortable Pace	▪ Slow ▪ Easy	▪ Fast ▪ Spontaneous	▪ Slow ▪ Systematic	▪ Fast ▪ Decisive
You'd Like Your Business Life to Be	▪ Personal ▪ Relaxed ▪ Friendly ▪ Informal	▪ Stimulating ▪ Social ▪ Active ▪ Fun	▪ Structured ▪ Organized ▪ Functional ▪ Detailed	▪ Busy ▪ Formal ▪ Efficient ▪ Productive
Preferred Social Distance	▪ < 3 feet	▪ < 3 feet	▪ > 3 feet	▪ > 3 feet
Your Least-Favorite Work Situation	▪ Confrontation	▪ Loss of prestige	▪ Being Embarrassed	▪ Loss of control
When You're Being Confronted, You Typically	▪ Acquiesce	▪ Get Sarcastic	▪ Withdraw	▪ Attack
You Enjoy	▪ Attention	▪ Recognition	▪ Accuracy	▪ Productivity
Your Primary Concern for Your Work Environment	▪ Close Relationships	▪ Flexibility	▪ Preparation	▪ Control
In a Work Environment, You Most Value	▪ Conformity ▪ Loyalty ▪ Compatibility with Others	▪ Playfulness ▪ Stimulation ▪ Recognition ▪ Discussion	▪ Correctness ▪ Thoroughness ▪ Precision ▪ Accuracy	▪ Leadership ▪ Competition ▪ Results ▪ Measurable Progress
You Want Others To Be	▪ Pleasant	▪ Stimulating	▪ Precise	▪ To the point
You Want To Be	▪ Liked	▪ Appreciated	▪ Correct	▪ In Charge
You're Uncomfortable Around	▪ Insensitivity ▪ Impatience	▪ Boredom ▪ Routine	▪ Surprises ▪ Lack of Clarity	▪ Inefficiency ▪ Indecision
Your Decision-Making Process is Typically	▪ Careful and Slow	▪ Spontaneous	▪ Researched	▪ Quick and Definitive
First Question: How An Event Will Impact	▪ Relationships	▪ Big Picture Plans	▪ Time to Completion	▪ Bottom Line

impact![32] I'll show you how to capitalize on your Action Types in the following chapters.

People-Oriented

Connector
You prefer an easy-going work environment that lets you take your time and get to know your customers. You excel at relationship-building.

Enthusiast
You do best when you can talk ideas through and lead others to execute your vision. You're a big-picture person and you excel at generating ideas.

Indirect ──────────┼────────── **Direct**

Thinker
You are detail-oriented and will do best in a work environment that lets you concentrate with limited distractions from people. You excel at precision and research.

Commander
You are a bottom-line, get-it-done person and you do best with goal-directed workaholics who get solid results in record time without guidance.

Task-Oriented

YOUR INTERNAL CLOCK

Most people have an on-off switch. At work, the switch is on. When they leave their job, the switch turns off and all thoughts of work are gone. It's playtime!

You and I are different. We never stop thinking, creating, imagining, envisioning and dreaming of ideas to make an impact. Our brains run 24/7 and we like it that way!

Family, friends and gurus say we should try to shut down. *"Take a break! Get your mind off of your work! It's good for you!"*

So you try.

Namaste. Breathe deeply and completely clear your mind…

---

32 If you currently hold a job that demands a lot of time outside your Happy Action Type, it's important you understand this is adding to your stress.

You close your eyes... You inhale... You exhale... Your muscles relax... Your mind quiets...

And suddenly appears the brilliant idea that had eluded you while you were distracted by all the shiny objects of your life.

YES! THAT WILL WORK!

Meditation is a beautiful thing! But do you celebrate your success? No! You feel like a meditation-dunce because you didn't clear your mind.

Stop trying to conform to the norm. You are a difference-maker! Celebrate your difference so you can capitalize on all life has to offer!

I invite you to embrace your brilliant, active mind and use it effectively by designing a 24-Hour Lifestyle that will allow you to take full advantage of your fabulous brain while capitalizing on all the wonderful experiences life has to offer you!

YOUR 24-HOUR LIFESTYLE

Divide your day into three segments:

UPTime is when you're actively interacting with people (not including family and friends). This includes everything from talking on the phone to engaging with the people you serve to chatting with a stranger at the grocery store.

DOWNtime is every moment you spend working on your business but where you aren't with people. This includes managing email, developing products and services, writing, strategic planning, bookkeeping, reading, education, research, etc.

MEtime is every moment you're not working in or on your business. This includes sleeping, eating, exercise, meditation, entertainment, time with family and friends and off-the-grid private time. Keep in mind, just because you're not consciously working in or on your business, unconsciously, your brain is active and the key is to let it happen without acting on it.

Your Ideal Lifestyle

24-Hour Impact

For now, design your lifestyle in three 8-hour segments. As you use this process, you'll discover the ideal number of hours for each segment based on what's best for you. The goal is to *actively choose* how you'll divide your time so you live your life by DESIGN (rather than by default).

One of the most important things to consider in your lifestyle design is travel. Specifically how far are you willing to travel to make your impact; how often are you willing to be away from home and for how long?

Another consideration is what you enjoy. Do you like writing? Speaking? Are you comfortable with technology or would you prefer to pay other people to manage that for you?

Everything you like and don't like goes into consideration when you design your working lifestyle and will be particularly important when it comes to developing and delivering your one-of-a-kind products and services (Chapter 7).

FOUR STEPS TO DESIGN YOUR IDEAL LIFESTYLE

Step 1: List Your Options

Make a list of every activity you currently do in your life and then add anything you think you might want to include in your ideal lifestyle. As you go, categorize each item according to Uptime, Downtime and Metime.[33]

Here are some examples of my clients' most popular choices:

UPtime (When you're actively interacting with people and making your impact)

- ✓ Speaking Live (locally, nationally and internationally)
- ✓ Speaking Virtually (webinars, teleseminars, hangouts, podcasts, videos)
- ✓ Coaching Live
- ✓ Coaching Virtually (phone or online)
- ✓ Consulting Live
- ✓ Consulting Virtually (phone or online)
- ✓ Service Consulting (helping people decide if your services are right for them)
- ✓ Retail Consulting (helping customers decide if your products are right for them)
- ✓ Networking Functions
- ✓ Networking by Phone
- ✓ Engaging with Strangers (from airports to grocery stores)
- ✓ Leadership (your team)
- ✓ Leadership (public or private meetings, workshops, retreats)
- ✓ Live Invitations (Presenting your products/services—in person or virtually—with an invitation for people to choose your products/services)
- ✓ Professional Development Conferences
- ✓ Personal Development Conferences
- ✓ Volunteer Work

---

33 I've created a Lifestyle Design Sheet for you. You can download it at FocusOnImpact.com/resources

✓ Shopping for Business (opportunity to impact strangers!)
✓ Playing with Colleagues and Team
✓ Outside Employment (all related activities associated with a job)

DOWNtime (When you work on your business and make your impact without actively interacting with people)[34]

✓ Writing (blogs, books, short articles, "white papers," impact emails)
✓ Marketing (invitation emails, autoresponders, websites, social engagement and creating/releasing your 60 Weeks of Impact[35])
✓ Product/Service development
✓ Bookkeeping
✓ Short-term and Long-term Planning
✓ Organization (aka clearing your desk!)
✓ Research
✓ Professional Development (reading, online training, offline training at home)
✓ Packing for Business-Related Travel

MEtime (When you do whatever you choose to do without working on or in your business)

✓ Sleeping
✓ Eating
✓ Entertainment at Home (T.V., music, games, movies, fun reading, chatting, texting, social emails, online play)
✓ Entertainment Outside (movies, concerts, live shows, restaurants)
✓ Shopping for Personal (opportunity to impact strangers!)
✓ Spiritual/Worship
✓ Exercise
✓ Meditation
✓ Personal Care (shower, etc.)[36]

---

34 No shaving, no makeup and no panty hose!
35 I'll teach you this in the City of Differentiate, Chapter 8.
36 Mani-Pedi's go here

- ✓ Cleaning[37]
- ✓ Laundry
- ✓ Gardening
- ✓ Caring for Family
- ✓ Playing with Family
- ✓ Playing with Friends
- ✓ Planning Vacations
- ✓ Packing for Vacations
- ✓ TAKING Vacations!

Step 2: Pick Your Favorites

Place a check next to each item on your list you would like to include in your lifestyle design and don't worry if you don't know how to make it happen. You can learn to do anything, and if it turns out it's not a good fit for you, simply erase it and choose something else. That's the beauty of designing your lifestyle—you get to pick!

Choose as many options as you like. The more you choose, the more flexibility you'll have in growing your impact in a way that fits your ideal lifestyle.

Step 3: Estimate Your Timing

For each item on your list, note your estimate of (1) how much time you will need to start and complete that activity (2) how much time you would need after each activity to clear your head, travel, etc., and (3) how many times per day, week, month or year you would want or need to engage in that activity.

For each activity you currently do in your life, notice how much time it's actually taking you (and prepare for a shock!). The most common mistake I see is underestimating how much time activities will take. This is the primary culprit that leads to being overwhelmed, exhaustion and lowered productivity. I learned the hard way to always leave a cushion of

---

37 Everything related to caring for home and family is considered "MEtime" because it is something you want done. That doesn't mean you have to personally do everything—only that you will allot time to do or delegate so your life is as you want it to be.

time between each activity I plan to allow for unexpected interruptions, challenges, and time to clear my head before the next activity.

Step 4: Design Your Balance

We've all got 24 hours per day, 7 days per week, 4-5 weeks per month and 52 weeks per year. The secret is to consciously design your lifestyle so you live the balance of UPtime, DOWNtime and MEtime that's best for you.

In Step 3, you listed your estimates for how much time you think each activity would take. Now, it's time to plug all of that into a design for your lifestyle.

For each item on your list, assign how many hours per day, week, month and year you would like to engage in that activity. When you're done, count up the hours for each day and make adjustments when you discover you're way over 24!

In the ideal world, your UPtime, DOWNtime and MEtime lists will be balanced into 8-hour segments while you're growing your business and weigh heavier on the MEtime as you grow your team. Realistically your life will vary and there will be many times during the year when your design will change for vacations, high-energy projects, multi-day projects, and special events.

The secret to designing and living your ideal lifestyle with balance is to give yourself permission to be flexible.

Regardless of how many responsibilities we have in our lives, balance depends on our ability to plan and our willingness to give ourselves permission to be flexible when life happens.

I had a perfectly balanced lifestyle, consciously designed so I could own and operate multiple businesses, engage in a social life, keep myself healthy and have fun! Then one day my mother called.

"The doctor took an x-ray and he found a spot on my lung. Can you come home?"

There are times in our lives when design goes out the window. I cleared my calendar for a week, made reservations and flew home to take my mom to the hospital for testing.

What began as a week turned into a sacred and horrible year of spending every moment of every day helping my mother fight a battle she couldn't win.

In the beginning I tried to work in the little room she used for her home office, running to her side whenever she needed me. But soon I was sleeping on hospital floors, sitting up with her all night long, driving her all over the countryside for appointments and using every moment she slept to research alternative cures.

Helpless, terrified and sleep-deprived, I became my mother's mother and cared for her the best I could. I was perpetually caught between wanting her to live forever and praying she'd be released from her pain. And on the night she died, I rocked her in my arms and reassured her as she took her last breath. It was Easter morning.

If you've ever lost someone you love, you know the deep, ache of longing for something you know you'll never have again. It's awful. It's relentless. It's exhausting.

It was a long time before I was ready to get back to my life and when I finally found the strength to start again I discovered a lot had changed in my absence. I had no regrets. I was deeply grateful to have had the privilege of being there for her and with her and wouldn't have given up one moment of the time we shared.

Now it was time to honor her gifts to me by spreading her impact through my own. It was time to rebuild and that meant starting over with a new plan and a new lifestyle design. The steps I'm teaching you here, along with the permission I gave myself to be flexible, turned out to be my greatest ally as I re-entered the business world. That, and my Focus On Impact.

As you design your lifestyle, be aware that we never know what could be around the bend. Make a commitment to yourself that you will give yourself permission to be flexible and then design your ideal lifestyle and live it to the max!

LOVE YOUR LIFE ALONG THE WAY

What I'm about to share with you is what my husband calls an "*obviousity*" —something that is so obvious, it's crazy to even bring it up![38]

**I believe the secret to loving your life
is to live your passion 24/7.**

As difference-makers, our passion is making an impact on people's lives. So why would we want to spend one moment of our lives doing anything less than making an impact?

When you let yourself live your passion, you discover new ways to make your impact every day.

Waiting in line at the grocery store? Why not turn to the stranger next to you and say something to get her laughing?

Talking on the phone to a customer representative at a utility company? Why not say something that will make his day?

Writing an email to your community? Forget selling and instead send practical information that will enhance their lives.[39]

Out for dinner with friends? Why not seize the moment to share an insight that could bring more joy to their lives?

Watching TV with your family? Enjoy the evening and permit your mind to wander anywhere it wants to go (including generating ideas for your next project).

Give yourself permission to enjoy life the way *you* want it to be. DESIGN your ideal lifestyle to capitalize on everything life has

---

38 "Obviousity" was recently listed in the Urban Dictionary, but I first heard it 30 years ago while enjoying a great cup of coffee with the man who became my husband. As far as I'm concerned, full credit for 'obviousity' goes to Dr. Hal Dibner, circa 1985.

39 See Chapter 8.

to offer and know that every moment is an opportunity for you to expand your impact.

When you Focus On Impact, life gets sweeter every day. Make your life everything you want it to be with Action Step # 5 and then turn the page for the City of DETERMINE!

ACTION STEP #5

Design Your Ideal Lifestyle!

Download your Lifestyle Design Planning Sheet at www.FocusOnImpact.com/resources and complete the **4 Steps to Design Your Ideal Lifestyle** described above.

For one week, keep track of everything you do and the amount of time you spend doing each thing. Get specific and leave *nothing* out. Then transfer your real-life times to the estimates you created above and adjust where needed.

Rate each item on your list according to how well it fits your Action Type on a scale of 1 to 5: 1 = not a fit, 2 = rarely a fit, 3 = sometimes a fit, 4 = nearly perfect, and 5 = a perfect fit.

In the ideal world, you would only engage in activities rated "5" – this is only possible if you have a team to support you. If you have a team, delegate all items rated "4" or less! If you don't have a team, schedule activities to capitalize on your brain-wiring as follows:

- Multi-task "1," "2" and "3" activities with "4" or "5" activities; or
- Separate "1," "2" and "3" activities from "4" or "5" activities with a 10-minute break to give your brain time to shift gears; or
- Schedule your "1," "2" and "3" activities for the morning and leave your "4" or "5" activities for the afternoon when you're likely to be slowing down.

The most important point of this Action Step is to make sure every area of your life is filled with impact-generating balance so you'll love your life all along your Journey of Impact and never lose sight of the passion that drives you.

The next step is to make sure your life is filled with wonderful people you'll love to serve! Let's make that happen in the City of DETERMINE![40]

---

40   This Action Step is one Enthusiasts and Commanders are likely to skip. *Please don't skip this or put it off!* Burnout is one of the leading causes of failure for difference-makers. If you take the time to design your lifestyle now, everything else in this book will be so much easier to implement!

Mult-Tasking for Action Types Combining activities to capitalize on your Action Types will help you love your life! Check the chart on Page 50 and make sure your Lifestyle Design is ideal for your unique Action Type. For example:

If you're an Enthusiast, folding laundry is not going to rate high on your Action Type scale. So, multi-task your laundry! Call a friend and make an impact in her day. Boring is now fun! Woo-hoo!

If you're a Thinker, you're likely to be uncomfortable attending a networking function. Combine your attendance with a research project where you conduct a detailed analysis of the people you meet and then provide your analysis to the organizer for future meetings. Your "1" becomes a solid "5."

The world is waiting for your impact. Turn the page for City # 4 of your Focus On Impact Map!

Chapter Six

DETERMINE YOUR PERFECT MARKET

***If one more marketing strategist tells me to
"narrow" my niche I'm going to scream!***

One of the first questions I ask my clients is, "*Who are the people you want to serve?*"

Inevitably they give me a demographic. "*Women aged 35—60*"... "*Fortune 100 companies*"... "*People who need to lose 20 lbs. or more*"...

Next I ask what makes them choose that particular niche.

"*They need my X.*"

"*Are they the only people who need your X?*" I ask.

"*Well, no. But aren't we supposed to narrow our niche?*"

Okay. With all respect, if that's what you believe, you've been *seminarized!* You've been to the webinars, read the books, heard the podcasts and clearly you drank the Kool-Aid®—and why wouldn't you?

Traditional business wisdom tells us, the more you narrow your niche, the more money you'll make. This is because the more you narrow your niche, the more defined your marketing conversation will be, and the more positively people will respond.

Traditional models also tell you to narrow your already "narrow niche" even further by seeking out "low hanging fruit"—the specific people who are ready to buy. And of course, traditional business models tell you to keep your pricing aligned with what your target market is proven to pay, run lots of sales, offer coupons, sink money into advertising and above all focus on ROI.[41]

To be clear, billions of dollars have been generated following this traditional approach because it works! Unless you're a difference-maker.

Difference-makers don't want to narrow our niche. And we shouldn't, because,

Narrowing your niche cheats people out of hearing about and being served by your impact!

So really, why would we narrow our niche? Just because tradition says we should? Or because it's easier? There's something really wrong with that! Why not find a way to market to *everyone* you want to serve and make *that* happen? It's time to *widen your niche!*

WHO IS IN YOUR PERFECT MARKET?

This may be one of the most important questions I'll ever ask you, so please take it very seriously. Here's a quick story to illustrate this crucial question.

During the first 20 years of my career I built several retail and service businesses serving a wide market. My clients and retail customers spanned every industry from healthcare to hair care and included politicians, corporate executives, solopreneurs, academicians, clinicians,

---

41 In case you're new to marketing, ROI = return on investment. The amount of money you put into marketing should be equal to or less than the money you make as a result.

non-profit staff and volunteers, artists, sales professionals, stay-at-home moms and MLM leaders.

I loved the variety of my consumer base! It made it possible for me to spread my impact around the globe and challenged me to constantly reinvent how I served my clients.

Then one day I got an invitation to speak to a group of 500 doctors who were clients of a major marketing firm specializing in healthcare. I was an accomplished speaker, but there was something about this particular event that fascinated me: These doctors were there because they were looking for help in growing their practices. This was all new to me, and I was really excited. Imagine the impact I could make if I helped all those doctors grow their impact!

I prepared more for that speech than I'd ever done, and the information I provided these doctors was unlike anything they'd ever heard. They were enthralled with the strategies I shared and when I got off the stage, they got out of their seats and followed me outside, ignoring the fact that another speaker had taken the stage.

Dozens and dozens of doctors surrounded me, competing for my attention, handing me their business cards and requesting private meetings. By the end of the day, my calendar was filled with consulting, executive retreats and training programs.

Word spread quickly about the success I brought my new clients and that launched a nine-year period where my company's niche increasingly narrowed to serving private practices and hospitals.

At first, I was thrilled. What better way to make a lasting impact than to serve people who heal people? It was an honor and a privilege—until it wasn't.

One day, my partner and I found ourselves conducting a retreat in the backwoods of a remote area. The program was supposed to be about providing better care for patients, but it quickly turned to something different. Several staff came to us during the first break to tell us about the *"abuse"* they were getting from their doctors. As it happened, the doctors overheard the discussion and quickly countered with stories about why their staff *"deserved what they got."*

That night, the managing partner invited us to his home so we could speak privately about the situation in his practice. His home was palatial and as we entered, I couldn't help but stare at the many animal heads hanging on his walls. He must have seen me staring because he invited us into another area of his home where he proudly revealed his *"Trophy Room"*—a 3000-square-foot ballroom filled edge-to-edge with enormous animals, staged in their natural habitats and posed in attack positions.

I excused myself and ran to the restroom.

Over the next few months, I thought a lot about that night and realized I'd been unhappy for a long time. Because while many of the doctors we'd served were wonderful, impact-driven professionals with great teams, they were the minority among the healthcare clients we'd served in the nine years that preceded that weekend.[42]

And while I fully sympathized with the new challenges facing doctors, and had helped make millions of dollars for those I'd served, I'd not realized the toll it had taken on me until that moment. It taught me a very powerful lesson:

Just because you can serve someone, doesn't mean you should.

Can we help people make money? Clearly. Is that the focus of our business? No. Our focus is on providing customized strategies to enable our clients to maximize and capitalize on their products and services. The substantial revenue growth they've seen has been the *direct result of* their impact.

The eye-opening epiphany of that experience led me to draw a clear line in the sand. I decided we would more carefully screen our inquiries

---

42 See Chapter 1 for my discussion on how healthcare shifted from a Focus On Impact to a focus on money and how it's affected doctors, patients and staff.

and would never again accept a client who came to us with the primary goal of getting rich.

Since then, the only doctors I serve are those who are driven to make a measurable difference in the lives of their patients, their partners and their staff. The only executives I help are those whose mission is to build an ever-growing impact—internally and externally. The only entrepreneurs I take on are those who are willing to challenge the status quo of business and turn full-focus on impact.

I consciously and purposefully chose my perfect market and my clients have reaped the benefits because now I genuinely *want* to spend more time with the people I serve. Of course, the more time we are together, the more I learn about them and the faster I can develop customized strategies for their culture, products and services. I respect my clients for their Focus On Impact and for their commitment to get measurable results—for the people they serve, for their teams and for themselves. Many of my clients have become close friends and I've had the privilege of witnessing how their *professional* impact has impacted their own *personal* lives.

What those clients have discovered is the same reality I discovered in my own businesses:

When you Focus on Impact—the money will come!

I widened my niche to include ALL difference-makers, regardless of their industry. Is that a niche? Absolutely. It's a really BIG niche, getting bigger every year as more and more people recognize that impact is the new currency and the most effective way to grow a business no matter what the product or service.

Now it's your turn. So once again… Who are the people you want to serve?

In today's market, your success depends on your ability to connect with people. The more real and vulnerable your conversations, the faster you'll build trust and the more your prospective customers will be driven to want more from you and your team. The simple truth is:

**The more you genuinely like and respect the people
in your market, the more your profits will soar.**

The first step is to DETERMINE the precise characteristics of the people you would *enjoy* serving. Who belongs in your market? Let's find out!

Imagine you were going to invite 12 people to your home for a dinner party. You can invite anyone you like (even if they lived centuries ago), as long as everyone on your list fascinates you in some way.

There is one rule: You have to spend the entire evening at the table listening to, and engaging with each of your guests (no hiding in the kitchen putting little decorations on desserts).

So, who is going to receive an invitation to your party? Once you've chosen your guests, make a list of the unique characteristics of each person including:

✓ Age
✓ Gender
✓ Education
✓ Values
✓ Special traits you like
✓ Socioeconomic status
✓ Business (include the industry[43])
✓ Expertise
✓ Primary position[44]
✓ Best known for
✓ What is it about this person that most fascinates you?
✓ What are this person's greatest challenges (in business or life)?

Congratulations! You've now defined the characteristics of your perfect market. You see, no matter what your message, product or service, your best market is going to be people you like to hang around, like to engage with and genuinely want to know better.

---

43 An industry is a general category of business such as engineering, entertainment, education, etc.
44 Primary position could be CEO, mother, student, etc.

In today's social world, your impact will grow exponentially the minute you realize you genuinely LIKE the people in your market!

When you like people, you'll look forward to serving them and they will respond to your genuine desire to know them. You'll love being with them (even if only virtually). They will feel your authentic desire to know them and be drawn to you as a result.

Of course, first you've got to find and attract them. I'll show you how to do that in the Action Step below and we'll discuss it in more detail in Chapter 8. For now, let's get clear on who you'll invite to your Table for 12 with Action Step # 6, and then you'll be ready for the City of DEVELOP.

ACTION STEP #6

Determine Your Perfect Market

Download your *Perfect Market Planning Sheet* at www.FocusOnImpact.com/resources and create the guest list for your dinner party. Note the personal and professional characteristics of each guest (you may need to do a little research).

If any of your guests lived long ago, translate their characteristics to today's world. For example, let's say you've chosen Martin Luther King, Jr. List all his characteristics, everything you can find out about him. Now find people in today's world whose traits are similar to those you most respect about him.

Next, determine the industries that would most likely attract people with those characteristics. Read blogs and search keywords that most closely describe what you like best about your guest (personally and professionally).

The important thing to remember is this:

Your market is not the people you invite to your party – Your market is everything and everyone those people represent.

Once you've determined your perfect market, add that to your Impact Action Formula, your unique gift and your ideal working lifestyle. This forms the foundation for your impact-driven business.

Now it's time to infuse all your uniqueness into your one-of-a-kind products and services. That happens in the City of DEVELOP! [45]

The world is waiting for your impact. Turn the page for City # 5 of your Focus On Impact Map!

---

45 Download your Perfect Market Planning Sheet at FocusOnImpact.com/resources. For larger organizations, get your marketing team to complete this Action Step and then collaboratively determine your perfect market by reaching consensus on your organization's Table for 12.

Chapter Seven

**DEVELOP
ONE-OF-A-KIND
PRODUCTS
AND SERVICES**

*How can I be sure what I send out
to the marketplace will be unique?*

When you're sitting alone in your office, it's hard to get a clear perspective on the unique impact you can bring to a crowded marketplace. So you go online, search keywords, discover the multitude of offerings in your product/service category, and get overwhelmed by the sheer volume of businesses you see.

The normal response is to become hopelessly discouraged. In fact, most people give up before they begin. But difference-makers don't give up—we get strategic.

Regardless of the quantity of options already available in your category, you'll have a distinct market advantage when you infuse your unique impact foundation into your products and services.

Your unmatchable contribution to the world (aka "unique selling proposition") will be easy to recognize and create once you've completed the Action Steps in the first four cities of your Focus On Impact Map. Again, these are:

Action Step 3: Define Your Impact Action Formula—gives you clarity regarding the unique, measurable impact you want to bring the world and what it will take to make that happen.

Action Step 4: Discover Your Unique Gift—gives you the steps to find your Seven-Factor Uniqueness by asking everyone who knows you one simple question.

Action Step 5: Design Your Ideal Lifestyle—assures whatever products/services you create will align with the lifestyle you want to live while you grow your impact.

Action Step 6: Determine Your Perfect Market—shows you how to identify and fully understand your Table for 12 Market to create the widest niche possible filled with people who will love everything you bring them.

Once you've completed those Action Steps, you'll have the foundation for developing your one-of-a-kind products and services.

The goal is to infuse your uniqueness into products/services that yield measurable results for the people who use them!

Let's look at how to make that happen.

YOUR PRODUCTS AND SERVICES

In the City of DEFINE, I showed you how to get crystal clarity on the impact you want to make by specifying what you want your buyers to DO, FEEL and HAVE *as a result of* using your products/services so you (and they) can measure the results of your impact.

When people get measurable results from your products/services, they experience something different than they've seen or felt before.

When you help them *watch* for the change that occurs, they will become *aware* of how your products/services impacted their life!

When consumers become aware of the difference you've made in their life, they use your products/services more often, get even bigger results and talk about it with their friends.

The fun really begins when you recognize your products/services can have multiple impacts! You see, while you may be focused on the ultimate impact, there are many smaller impacts that will happen on the way there and afterwards!

When you figure out all those little steps that add up to—and result from—your ultimate impact, you'll be ready to create an entire suite of products/services, each of which will deliver a new piece of impact that picks up where the last left off. You'll then offer each of those in a cumulative order so each product/service people buy yields an impact (a measurable result) that then entices them to want more.

I call that *Sequencing Your Impact.* It's a lot like getting into an unheated pool in early spring. Some people are fearless and jump right in. Yes, they're chilly, but they start swimming and quickly adjust to the temperature. These are the customers who will likely go straight for your ultimate impact product/service and never look back.

The vast majority of adults don't jump into a pool. They gingerly put one toe into the water, pull it back out and then slowly lower their entire foot onto the first step, squealing while they adjust to the temperature of the water. They balance there for a moment or two and then slowly introduce their second foot. Standing motionless on the safe step, they call out,

You go ahead! I just want to breathe in this amazing day.

Inspired by the vision of their friends splashing in the water, they lower themselves one more step, where they remain for a few more minutes. Step by agonizing step, they work their way into the pool, where they stand on tip toes with arms way above their head, struggling to keep their upper body from getting wet. Soon they get lonely watching their friends enjoy the pool, and at last they muster the courage to go all-in so they too can join in the fun.

Every time you introduce a new product/service, your market will be filled with *Tip-Toers*. The more unique and/or expensive your product/ service, the more they will choose to go in one toe at a time and the more they'll need social proof of the impact you provide. You can accelerate the process of turning your *Tip-Toers* into *Divers* by *Sequencing Your Impact*. Here's how:

4 STEPS TO SEQUENCE YOUR IMPACT

Step 1: Look closely at the ultimate impact you want to make for your buyer—specifically, what do you want people to be able to do, be or have after they have purchased and used your product/service. We'll call that your *ultimate impact*.[46]

> *Example*: You are a realtor. The ultimate impact you want to bring to people is *the pride they'll feel when they take ownership of their new home and the joy they'll experience as they create lasting memories there.*

Step 2: Now take a step back and reverse-engineer your ultimate impact from Step 1. What would people have to be, *do, know* or *have* before they would be *able* or *willing* to experience your ultimate impact?

> *Example*: Before they can own a home, they have to buy a home. So the impact you want to create is *an easy purchasing experience that fills your customer with confidence that they made the right choice and can comfortably handle their mortgage payments.*

Step 3: Now back up one step further and figure out what they would have to be, *do, know* or *have* before they would be *able* or *willing* to experience the impact from Step 2.

> *Example*: Before they can have an easy purchasing experience, they have to choose the perfect home for their needs and

---

46   If you're still not sure, revisit the City of DEFINE in Chapter 3.

wants. So the impact you would want to create is *a fun and well-orchestrated experience looking at houses that generates happy, stress-free memories they'll associate with the care you provided.*

Step 4: Repeat Step 3 four more times to create a total of six impacts (including your ultimate impact).[47] Remember, you are reverse-engineering. So each impact leads to the next, ending with your ultimate impact.

You take all of these details for granted. You're ready to dive right in. But for those of us who live outside of your world, we appreciate the one-toe-in-the-water approach to your impact.

DEVELOP **One-Of-A-Kind Products/Services**

Ultimate Impact →

Initial
x
Impact

What Are Your Impact Ripples?

If you're not sure how to figure out your sequence, go directly to the people you want to serve and ask them for input.

Nothing will increase your impact faster (and lead to higher sales of your products/services) than going directly to the people you want to serve and getting their input through effective research.

---

47   There's no rule that says you have to have six ripples, but my experience is that number produces powerful results.

Every product/service I've ever created began with research. That's how I developed my credo, *"Sell it first, then create it!"*

Here's how to use effective research to sequence your impact so you can develop a full suite of products/services *and* make a measurable impact in people's lives:

Begin by defining your ultimate impact—what people will be able to be, do or have as a result of experiencing your product/service. Then reach out to those who match the characteristics of your Table for 12 Dinner Party through social media, in speaking engagements, through online surveys and in face-to-face interviews.

Keep your research simple and short by inviting people to help you by responding to one question. Your question will follow this formula:

If you could [insert the ultimate impact of using your product/service], **specifically how would that affect every area of your life?**

For example, let's say you're a financial advisor and you want to help people keep more of their money so they can do more of what they love. So you might post,

I need your help with a quick research project. Please answer this question (thanks, in advance, for your help): If you knew how to keep more of the money you make, specifically how would that affect all the areas of your life?

Collect and analyze their responses. What you'll have is a precise list of what they want in their lives. Now, use the 4 Steps to Sequence Your Impact and reverse engineer until you have a total of SIX measurable impacts. Each impact will be the result of a one-of-a-kind product or service you will create.

Do you really need to go through all of this to develop your one-of-a-kind products/services? Let's look at a quick metaphor:

Imagine it's summertime and you're getting ready to attend a conference at a big convention center. The forecast is hot and humid with thunderstorms predicted for the afternoon. You want to be comfortable, but the dress code is "business casual" and you want to make a good impression.

As you stand in your closet surveying your choices, you remember the last event you attended there when the air conditioning was so freezing you could barely feel your feet!

You select a shirt, pants, blazer and shoes. For the cold auditorium, a pullover sweater that fits under the blazer and a raincoat for the afternoon.

Hmmm...I'm forgetting something...Oh!

You pull open a drawer, grab undergarments and start getting dressed—undergarments first, then shirt, pants, shoes and blazer. You carry the sweater and raincoat on your arm for later and you're ready to go.

Note: You take this process for granted—but it is the key to product development!

There is a *sequence* to how you get dressed. Each piece of your outfit goes on one layer at a time, in a sequenced order that enables you to get maximum benefits from each piece of clothing. If you put the clothes on out of order, you're likely to get some very strange glances at the conference and, while you'll certainly make an impression, it probably won't be the one you wanted. So you dress sequentially, and the cumulative result gives you everything you want.

Developing your products/services follows the same sequential necessity because we need to be fully prepared in order to appreciate the ultimate impact you want us to receive. Here's how:

PRODUCT SEQUENCING

Each impact you've specified in your 4 Steps to Sequence Your Impact will be *the result of* a one-of-a-kind product/service you develop and offer in *sequence*.

Product sequencing is the process of developing one-of-a-kind products and services that sequentially build a cumulative impact.

Each product/service you develop leads to—or is associated with—the next in a natural sequence based upon the impact you want to make in your market. Each stands alone and complements the others. The more you develop, the greater your impact, the faster your reputation will spread and the more impact you'll experience in your own life (and bank account!).

The best way I can explain this is to give you an example. Following is an edited transcript from a client coaching session:

Me: *What is the ultimate impact you want to bring to your Table-for-12 market?*

Client: *I want my market to live well into their 90's with full vitality, function and joy.*

Me: *Okay, cool! So now, what are five impacts you'll have to make first—before they'll be open and ready to receive your ultimate impact?*

Client: *First, they'd need to feel the need for this—so that means they have to feel bad that they're lacking vitality, function and joy now!*

Me: *What kind of "bad" do they need to feel—sad, mad, embarrassed, scared?*

Client: *Maybe all of it.*

Me: *Good. And what are the other four impacts?*

Client: *They need to experience what "vitality" is like before they can want it and then number three would be to decide what "function" means for them… then I think they need to know how to feel "joy" no matter what happens but before all that they need to develop and sustain a determination to live fully into their 90's.*

Me: *Great! What categories of products and services have you chosen for your Ideal Lifestyle and what's your top DESIRE for your impact?*

Client: *I want to speak, to do retreats, and to have both an online retail store with advertisers and a limited coaching service of no more than three hours per week. I also want to travel to exotic places at least once a month. And I want to reach one million people with my message in the next two years so I can create a movement.*

Me: *On a scale of 1—10, how badly do you want this?*
Client: *47.*
Me: *Do you have a complete list of all the RESOURCES you'd need to be able to achieve your DESIRES?*
Client: *Yes* [client emailed the list and I confirmed].
Me: *What's your expertise?*
Client: *I've got a degree in fitness and nutrition and I've coached over 100 people as a personal trainer.*
Me: *What is the Unique Gift you bring to the table?*
Client: *I've been told I have an unusual ability to help people feel younger. I guess that's true because men and women who are over 50 tell me they feel like they're 25—and that usually happens in only three sessions. But I'm not sure how to do that outside of a personal training situation in other products and services.*
Me: *Here's an example of how this could work: Your initial impact could be delivered through paid speaking engagements where you would help the audience develop a determination to live fully into their 90's. With your speech, you'd provide a guidebook with a practical, step-by-step Action Plan to sustain that determination. Your guidebook would state your commitment to provide ongoing support on a social platform that will be open to the public so others see the coaching you're doing there.*
Client: *Love it.*
Me: *You can also video your speech and then offer that video with your guidebook as a complimentary gift on a lead generation page where people enter their names and email addresses and get free access to both. This will grow your email list and you can serve them with your 60 Weeks of Impact* [48] *to keep them engaged.*
Client: *This is awesome.*
Me: *Your next product would be a bestselling book where you'll give all the practical steps and inspiration they need to experience the impact you provided in your speech, plus four more pieces of impact. You'll entice them to implement by telling them what they have to look forward to after they follow all the practical steps you*

---

48   I'll teach you all about 60 Weeks of Impact in the next chapter.

gave them in the book. Then, at the back of the book you'll invite them to attend your next exotic retreat where they'll discover how to live well into their 90's with full vitality, function and joy.

Client: *WOW.*

Me: *At the retreat you'll offer private coaching and since your lifestyle design doesn't allow for more than three hours a week of that, you'll have to find a way to fast-track the results you deliver, or else you can choose selection criteria people have to pass to be allowed to enter your coaching program. Of course, you can also set a fee that's out of reach for most people.*

Client: *I like the challenge of three-hour fast-track. I'm getting more ideas too. DVDs, membership site…*

Me: *There's no limit—just make sure each product is sequenced to bring the impact you want them to get in the order you want them to get it.*

Got it? There is no limit to what you can develop when you let your creativity loose and capitalize on all your uniqueness. Just remember:

It's not about the impact you want to make.
It's about creating the impact people want to get.

So let's review:

Step 1: Review your Foundation of Uniqueness Look at your responses to Action Steps 3–6 and use them to define the types of products/services you want to develop and the unique gift you'll infuse to make everything you create your one-of-a-kind offering to the world.

Step 2: Sequence Your Impact by identifying the five measurable impacts you'll make that will lead up to your ultimate impact.

Step 3: Sequence Your Products For each impact you've identified, develop a product or service that will lead your market to experience that impact.

Please don't think you need to develop all of your products/services at once! Start with the one furthest away from your ultimate impact and get that out into the market place.

Always follow up with buyers to research the impact you brought to their life by asking them to measure the results they got from their experience with you.

The data you collect from your buyers will be the best marketing tool you'll ever find. Be sure to combine rating questions (*On a scale of 1 to 5...*) with open-ended questions (*How would you describe...*) so you'll have quotable testimonials.

You can also invite your buyers to send you a quick video sharing specifically how your product/service impacted their life. This is social proof at its finest! And remember the ripple effect!

Each product/service your consumer buys and uses will bring results that lead to a ripple effect of impact!

As you witness the ripple effect of your impact, you'll get new ideas for products/services you can develop to serve your market!

Of course, to make all of that happen, you've got to develop your first product/service!

Where will you begin? Let's find out with Action Step # 7 and then I'll share with you the most powerful process I've ever found to spread your impact around the globe in the City of DIFFERENTIATE!

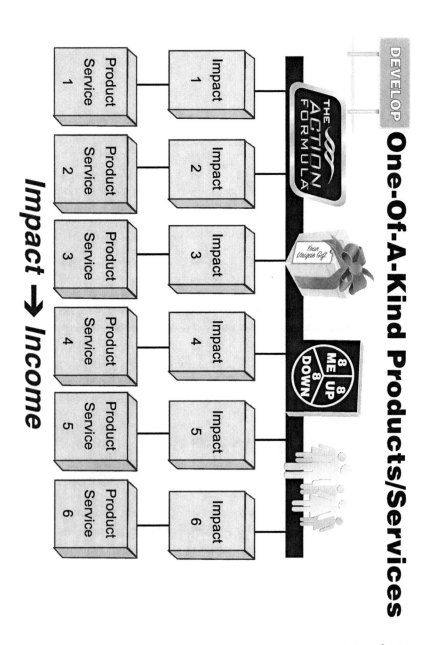

One-Of-A-Kind Products/Services

DEVELOP

THE ACTION FORMULA

Your Unique Gift

8 ME UP
8 8
DOWN

Product Service 1	Product Service 2	Product Service 3	Product Service 4	Product Service 5	Product Service 6
Impact 1	Impact 2	Impact 3	Impact 4	Impact 5	Impact 6

Impact → Income

ACTION STEP #7

Develop One-Of-A-Kind Products & Services

Clear off your desk or table top and lay out four pages side by side:

Your Impact Action Formula Planning Sheet, Unique Gift Discovery Sheet, Lifestyle Design Planning Sheet and Perfect Market Planning Sheet.

Under that, lay out six blank pages side by side.

On the first page, list your Ultimate Impact and then on the remaining five pages create your Sequence of Impact - one impact per page.

Below each of your six IMPACT pages, lay another blank page. Each of these six pages represents a product or service you will develop to create the IMPACT you've identified in the page above.

Sequence your products from the beginning of the Sequence to the end and develop each product by infusing your unique Impact Action Formula, Unique Gift, Unique Lifestyle and Unique Market.

Note: The hardest part of this is thinking through the Sequence of Impact. Once you've got that figured out, you're ready to develop your one-of-a-kind products and services.

The next step is to make sure people find you and choose you! That happens in the City of DIFFERENTIATE! [49, 50]

The world is waiting for your impact. Turn the page for City # 6 of your Focus On Impact Map!

---

49 In order to fully capitalize on this Action Step, I suggest you complete Action Steps 3 – 6 so you have the clarity you need for your Foundation of Uniqueness.

50 Need help thinking it through? Join the conversation at Facebook.com/focusonimpact and ask for help identifying your Sequence of Impact! Everyone in the Community of Difference-Makers is blind to your impact so they will make this easier for you by asking questions. And please remember to be there for others when they ask for help! Together our impact will be far greater than any we will ever create alone!

Chapter Eight

DIFFERENTIATE
WITH IMPACT-DRIVEN MARKETING

In our crowded global marketplace, impact is the currency that establishes your brand as the go-to resource for your products and services!

How can you get people to choose you above everyone else in your industry?

How can you get your message heard if you have no advertising budget?

How can you get strangers to track you down to find out what they can buy from you?

How can you get invitations for speaking engagements and media interviews?

And how do you make all of that happen in a global market where consumers are bombarded by too-good-to-be-true promises, where price trumps quality and where social proof is more credible than anything? The answer is:

Capitalize on the Era of Entitlement

When I was little, my mother would go to the delicatessen and while she was placing her order, a nice man would hand me a pretzel that looked like a cigar and say, *"This is for you, Wendy, because you're such a good girl!"*

Fifty miles away, my grandmother shopped at her favorite grocery store where the man behind the counter called her by name and gave her *a little slice to taste.*

In the 60's, courtesy sampling was a special treat reserved for treasured customers. Today, sampling has become commonplace, leading consumers to believe they're entitled to receive free samples of all products and services.

Want something for free? Just go to the app store! Visit any major grocery store in the U.S. on a weekend and by the time you've gone up and down the aisles, you'll have tasted so many samples, you'll be too full for dinner! Go to a department store and, when you least expect it, someone will pop in front of you and spritz a free sample of cologne right in your face. Stroll a bit further and get a free makeover from any cosmetic brand you choose and get samples of skin care to try at home. Visit iTunes and sample the music you want to buy before you commit to your purchase. Try a new bed for an entire week before you decide if you like it.

Buy one, get one free—PLUS get a free XYZ and our no-hassle returns policy! Don't like it? No problem! Just bring it back and you can even keep the special XYZ bonus just for trying it today!

"Try before you buy" defines our global economy.

Welcome to the Era of Entitlement where consumers expect you to give something for free. But don't despair…this is fabulous news for you! The pretzel I accepted way back when set up a culture where you can capitalize on the habit that is most familiar to shoppers today.

The strategic process I'm about to show you will turn your marketing into a relationship-building power tool! Get ready to grow a loyal community of people who will click, like and share your impact around the globe—without spending a penny to make it happen!

I first discovered the process I'm about to show you when I went to a business networking event. They invited me to talk about my business and instead, I stood up and gave a 10-minute speech on the science of capitalizing in a social setting. When I finished, I was surrounded by people and one had a credit card in her hands.

"I don't know what you sell, but whatever it is, I want some."

All I'd done was present how-to tips—information that would be helpful to them. I never once mentioned my business. I was focused on helping them right there in that moment and since I had no earthly idea who these people were, I went for the one thing I knew they all needed: networking tips.

I walked away with dozens of cards and a wonderful new friend. Martie (the credit card woman) became my best customer and the referrals she sent me covered my monthly expenses for three years!

As time went by, I tested lots of different formulas for marketing. I wrote articles for industry journals and magazines, presented at conferences, sent direct mail pieces and kept track of all my results. Then one day, I delivered the keynote speech at an ultra-conservative conference in Dallas, TX. Afterwards a group of people rushed the stage to talk to me and one handed me a check. At the time, I thought it was my speaking fee and I just thanked him and put it in my jacket pocket.

He waited while I finished talking with everyone, followed me out of the ballroom and caught up with me at the door to the restroom.

"Did you look at the check?" he asked.

"No I haven't had a chance, but thank you so much for having me today!" I replied quickly.

His eyes were glaring at me and I was starting to get nervous. *"Look at the check and then tell me what you think,"* he commanded.

I reached in my pocket and retrieved the folded check. When I opened it I saw a signature but there was no amount written. *"I don't understand. What is this?"* I asked.

"Look," He whispered, *"I have no idea what you do but you're the first person today who has made any sense. My business is in trouble. Whatever it costs, I think you're the one to help me."*

I had found the formula. And now I'm going to share it with you. It all begins with one truth:

Give more than you get and you'll get more than you ever dreamed possible!

Instead of using marketing as a vehicle to inform your market about what they can buy from you, show them what they can *experience with you.* Commit all your marketing to serving up information in ongoing Impact Gifts that help people live better, safer, happier, healthier and more fulfilling lives. Master this, and you'll do more than differentiate your brand—you'll become the premier provider for your products and services.

What I'm about to share with you is a marketing process that will make it possible for you to attract, convert and serve everyone you want to reach without sleazy sales campaigns and without spending one penny on advertising. I developed, tested and used this unique process to grow my own businesses and then passed it on to my clients across multiple industries, helping them grow their impact and bring in seven-figure revenues during the worst and best of economic conditions.

This is marketing at its finest—it's powerful, it's internationally proven and it's easy! So let's go…

A NEW KINGDOM

For years we've been told *Content is King!* I'm here to tell you times have changed. Today there are way too many kings creating so *much* content, consumers are overwhelmed and content-weary.

Today's consumers want short, practical, how-to tips they can use to solve their problems fast! They don't want information. They want *measurable results*! In the new global kingdom,

Impact is King!

You'll rule the kingdom when you offer easy-to-create, short, content pieces that deliver a measurable impact. And here's the best part: If you use the strategy I'm about to show you to create your content, you'll be able to develop an entire year of powerful impact-driven marketing and deliver it with minimal investment of time!

60 WEEKS OF IMPACT

The first step is to research "*how-to*" and "*what is*" questions people are entering into major search engines that are *related to* your products and services. Please note the emphasis in that sentence. We're not looking for questions they're asking *about* your products/services. We're looking for questions about things that are *indirectly related* to your products/services.[51]

For example:

If you're the author of a cookbook, your market is searching for answers about food, lifestyle cooking, cooking utensils and dietary concerns.

If you're an internet-law attorney, related questions include app development, merchant accounts and internet marketing.

If you sell swimming pools, your market is looking for tips on aquatic exercise, outdoor furniture, water safety and outdoor parties.

---

51 As you type words into a search engine, the most frequently entered searches appear immediately below the search box. For example, type the word "how" and the first sentence that pops up is "*how to tie a tie*." Each additional word you add will change the search engine response. For more online search ideas, go to FocusOnImpact.com/resources.

Think about everything people would need or want before, during and after they consume your product/service. Search accessories, experiences and design. The more you expand your perspective around what you have to offer, the more people you'll attract who are interested in what you offer.

Now you're ready to create your impact-driven marketing! Simply follow these steps:

5 STEPS TO CREATE IMPACT-DRIVEN MARKETING[52]

Step 1: Searchable Questions. Make a list of the Top 10 questions people might search related to your message, products or services. *How do I...*

Step 2: Easy Answers. For each of the 10 questions, create a quick, bottom-line answer—*Do this, don't do that.*

Step 3: Practical Tips. For each of your bottom-line answers, list three practical tips people can do immediately to get results. Hint: make them simple and actionable. *First do this, then do this, then do this.*

Step 4: Expand Your Impact. For each of the 10 questions (and associated set of practical tips), list five follow-up questions people might ask that would enable them to go deeper into what you've already shown them. *Now that you know how to do A, you might be wondering, "How do I do B, C, D, E and F?"*

Step 5: Follow-Up Gifts. For each of the five questions you listed in Step 4, create a new content piece, addressing each question with one easy answer and three practical tips people can do right away to get fast results. *Last week I showed you how to X. So the next question we need to look at is, how can you do Y?*

PACKAGE YOUR GIFTS

Each Impact Gift you create will be packaged in a short content piece (approximately 400—500 words (2.5—4 minutes of audio or video). To put content together that will serve your market and move them

---

52 To download your personal *60 Weeks of Impact Planning Sheet*, go to FocusOnImpact.com/resources.

to action, use the following formula and turn your content into game-changing results for the people you serve—and for you!

7 STEPS TO CREATE IMPACT-DRIVEN C. O. N. T. E. N. T.

Step 1: Connect with credibility. Introduce yourself by giving your name, and two or three things about you that will help us see you as an authority.

> **Hint**: One of the items on your list should be searchable so we can do our research and assure ourselves you are someone we want to know.

Step 2: Open the conversation. Ask the question you're about to answer.

> **Hint**: As you ask the question, reflect the tone they hear inside their heads when they ask *themselves* this very same question! The closer you come to understanding and mirroring their emotions, the faster you'll send the message that you really empathize with their pain.

Step 3: Normalize the problem. Give a statistic or tell a story to show they are not alone in experiencing this problem.

> **Hint**: One of the greatest impacts you'll ever make is when you help people know they aren't alone. Be reassuring and free them with facts.

Step 4: Teach practical tips. Walk them step-by-step through the three tips you've created to solve at least a portion of the problem.

> **Hint**: For each tip, give the bottom line first and then a quick explanation or example to help them get what you're telling them to do.

Step 5: Entice them to implement. This is where the power of your impact takes hold! Help them envision what life would be like if they implemented your advice and reaped the rewards of the change they've made.

Hint: Paint a vivid picture by sharing a true story that happened to you or someone who has used your products/services. Keep it real. Avoid phrases like, *"Just imagine if..."* Let the story do the job for you.

Step 6: Nurture their curiosity. Now that you've solved *that* problem, let them know you understand there are other questions that could come up for them. Amaze them with your foresight and share the five important questions they need to know, then promise you'll be back to give them practical tips for all five questions over the next five weeks.

> **Hint**: When you list the five questions, excite them about getting those answers by sharing a preview of what they have to look forward to (what life will be like once they know how to solve those five challenges).

Step 7: Tie it all together with 3 invitations and 1 message. End your content piece by inviting them to (1) share stories of how they used your tips, (2) post other questions they'd like answered and (3) come to your website for more free tips.[53] Then share a simple message to tie it all together.

> **Hint**: Your message is not a marketing tag line. It's a lesson you've learned in your life that means something to you. This is the icing on the cake that makes your Impact Gift personal and meaningful for your market. Always use the same message for continuity and branding.[54]

Connect with credibility

Open the conversation

Normalize the problem

Teach practical tips

Entice them to implement

---

53   To monetize this powerful marketing process, see Chapter 9.
54   For a tutorial on how to find your unique message, go to FocusOnImpact.com/
resources

Nurture their curiosity

Tie it all together 3:1

The C.O.N.T.E.N.T. Formula is the most powerful process I've ever created for impact-driven marketing.[55] Notice there is no selling at all in your Impact Gifts. You introduce your searchable information at the start and close with an invitation for more free gifts. Your marketing gifts are about impact—genuine service to differentiate you from all of the sales-driven marketing that's out there. When you Focus On Impact—the money will come!

I've built all of my businesses using this formula. Here are just some of the thousands of social comments I received the first time I sent out a complimentary video series online using the C.O.N.T.E.N.T. Formula,

- *I feel like I've known you all my life!*
- *It's like you always know exactly what I'm thinking.*
- *Thank you for everything you've brought to my family's life.*
- *You've given us information other people charge 10's of 1000's for!*
- *Where can I learn more about your services?*
- *Do you have a book or CD I can buy?*
- *You give so much. What can I do for YOU?*

And the one that brought me to my knees,

- *I want you to know, you just saved my life.*

Never underestimate the power of your impact.

The more gifts you give, the more you'll receive. It's the natural result of impact. So the next question you might be asking is:

Where do I put all these impact gifts so people will find me, follow me, choose me and send all their friends to me?

The answer is: Everywhere!

---

55 For fabulous information to help you increase your visibility as a thought leader, meet Forbes contributor, PR Expert and my dear friend, Cheryl Snapp Conner at FocusOnImpact.com/resources.

It's time for you to capitalize on the marvel of our world, a market where you can reach billions of people with a single click.

SEND YOUR IMPACT GIFTS AROUND THE GLOBE!

Look closely at the **FOI Platform Power Map** below. This map represents the most exciting differentiation strategy I've ever found. Here's how it works:

Platform 1: Create your 400-word Impact Gift using the C.O.N.T.E.N.T. Formula.

> **Hint:** Write your 400-word piece as if you were having a conversation. I've been doing this with you throughout this book. I see you sitting right where you are, holding this book in your hands. The words on this page are exactly as I'd speak if you were sitting right here next to me—and that's critically important with impact-driven marketing. It has to be your authentic voice so we can connect to and develop trust for YOU.

Platform 2: Upload your 400-word C.O.N.T.E.N.T. to a teleprompter or use a big flip chart with an outline to guide you for main points you want to make and then record a 2–3 minute video.

> **Hint:** Video is an intimate conversation between two people. Simply look into the camera and talk to one of the people at your Table for 12. See him/her sitting right there in the lens. Don't perform. Enjoy your dinner conversation. If you're not comfortable speaking in front of a video, create some slides and do a voiceover. The point is to connect and serve.[56] Then upload your video to YouTube® and other video platforms with a searchable title about the question your video addresses.[57] Remember to upload the transcript of your video (your 400-word C.O.N.T.E.N.T.) to the backend in the Closed Captions for the Hearing Impaired section.

Platform 3: Upload the 400-word C.O.N.T.E.N.T. to your blog, tweak it for articles in online and offline publications, send the tips in an email to your community and share on social media platforms frequented by your Table For 12.

> **Hint:** Never upload precisely the same content on multiple online sites. Be sure to add approximately 1/3 new content (a new opening, new example or new closing) so search engines don't flag anything as plagiarism. Social platforms will challenge your creativity. Break up your Impact Gift into multiple tweets. Grab a screenshot from your video for Pinterest®. Remember, social media sites are designed to be, well, *social.* So have fun with this and above all, invite engagement with questions so people will connect with you!

---

56   Consider royalty-free music and branded logo openings ("bumpers") for extra pizazz and viewer engagement. For free training on video production and to meet the people I recommend for my video production needs, go to FocusOnImpact.com/resources

57   Popular video platforms beyond YouTube® shift regularly and new sites pop up every day. Do your research to find the sites your market frequents for information and entertainment and be there waiting for them when they arrive!

Platform 4: Strip the soundtrack from your video and make the audio available as a downloadable MP3 on your site, and as a podcast.

> **Hint:** Keep the music for your opening and closing, but remove background music while you're speaking.

Platform 5: Send the question you're addressing, and an easy answer for each of your three tips to radio, television and print media producers with a catchy "hook" in your subject line connecting your topic to a current hot topic.[58]

> **Hint:** Serving on radio, TV and in print media is a lot of fun, it's lifestyle-friendly and the exponential reach it can give you is extraordinary. Just stick to your C.O.N.T.E.N.T. formula and you'll do great!

Advanced Platforms: Combine several impact gifts and offer webinars, teleseminars, Hangouts and Meetups. Publish a bestselling e-book and when you're ready, publish your content in paperback or hardcover edition. Share your Impact Gifts in speaking engagements and get paid top fees to spread your impact around the globe in beautiful venues.[59]

> **Hint:** Consult your *Lifestyle Planning Sheet* before making a decision about which of these platforms to choose. I've had the privilege of speaking around the globe for hundreds of thousands of people, and I can tell you there is nothing that will ever match the feeling you'll get when you're standing in a room, looking out at the people you've come to serve. In addition to the joy you'll experience being face-to-face with people who need your help, the financial rewards for your impact can be substantial. On the other hand, if your Lifestyle Plan keeps you close to home, or you don't want to be on stages, you can serve around the globe through the online platforms. It's truly up to you and the lifestyle you've designed. Above all—love your life!

---

58   For tips and resources to get free publicity through radio, TV and print media, visit www.FocusOnImpact.com/resources

59   See Pages 185 – 190 for discounted access to live and online training to help you grow your business through speaking.

Your impact will be felt most where you are most comfortable!

All that exposure out of only 400 words! And the best part is, it doesn't matter where you begin! Not ready to do videos? No problem! Start with blogs and audios. Want to travel? Start by speaking and then record and transcribe your speeches.

There is no limit to what you can accomplish when you forget traditional marketing strategies and Focus On Impact! Start now with Action Step # 8 and then I'll show you how to turn your impact into revenue in the City of DELIVER.

ACTION STEP #8

Differentiate With Impact-Driven Marketing

Sending out your Impact Gifts will be one of the most exciting things you'll ever do to build and grow your impact-driven business.

Set aside one hour per day for one week so you can research the key questions your Table for 12 market is asking about topics that are related to your products/services.

Go to www.FocusOnImpact.com/resources and download your personal *60 Weeks of Impact Planning Sheet.* Then create your 10 questions, 10 easy answers, three practical tips, five follow-up questions and associated three tips per question.

Use the C.O.N.T.E.N.T. Formula to write an Impact Gift for the first question.

Choose three platforms on the Focus On Impact Platform Power Map and launch your first Impact Gift!

Repeat until you've completed your 60 Weeks of Impact. Then start again!

The next step is to maximize and capitalize on your impact by delivering your products and services so they move people to action! That happens in the City of DELIVER!

The world is waiting for your impact. Turn the page for City # 7 of your Focus On Impact Map!

Chapter Nine

DELIVER YOUR IMPACT AND MOVE PEOPLE TO ACTION

Impact is the result of ethical influence.

From the alarm that wakes you in the morning to the person who kisses you goodnight, everything and everyone in your life is there because something *outside you* connected with something *inside you* to move you to action.

If you were to trace back every choice you've ever made, from the food you eat to the clothes you wear to the chair you're sitting in at this very moment…

If you were to analyze everything that went through your mind as you moved from *discovery* of a need/want to *choosing* a thing/person to fulfill your need/want to *taking actions* to get that thing/person into your life to actively *using* that thing/person to *getting results from* that thing/person to *telling others* about that thing/person …

In other words, if you figured out everything that moved you to action in every choice you've ever made, you'd know a lot about influence!

If you were then to take it further and study the factors that move *other* people to action, you'd learn even more about influence.

I know, because that's precisely what I did...I figured out what moved *me* and went on to study everything I could get my hands on to learn what moved other people to action!

I first discovered the power of influence at a very early age. The only child of a single mother, our apartment in New York City was a den of influence. My mom would coax me to what she wanted me to do and I would try to influence her to let me do whatever I wanted (inevitably the opposite of her desires).[60]

Influence is part of everyday life, though not all influence is ethical.

Where influence is about getting people to do what you want them to do, ethical influence demands we focus on helping people get what they want while following a defined set of Ethical Pillars.[61]

The first time I discovered the extraordinary power of using ethical influence to make an impact on people's lives was in 1976, when I got a summer job working as a counselor at a camp for overweight girls.

My vision of an "easy summer" was quickly squashed when I found myself responsible for 10 cranky pre-teens who spent all their time finding ways to get into trouble. I'd tried everything I could think of to get these girls to follow the camp guidelines, but nothing worked.

After two weeks of endless frustration, my mother drove up to sweep me away for my first day off. As we strolled the tourist shops of Nantucket, I shared story after story about my campers. She walked silently beside me, all the while beaming with a knowing smile.

"Okay, mom, I get it. This is exactly what I did to you. A million apologies!" I sighed.

---

60   To this day, I marvel at my mother's brilliance as a master of influence, and the patience she showed as I exerted my DNA-driven right as a teenager to surpass my loving teacher.

61   For more on Ethical Pillars, see Chapter 3.

She put her arms around me and in her best motherly tone assured me, *"You know exactly how to handle these girls and they're lucky to have you."* As I nestled my head on her shoulder, I saw a big sign that said, *Custom T-Shirts.*

"That's it!" I screamed.

We ran inside and while my mom browsed hundreds of shells painted with beach scenes, I bought 10 extra-extra-large, neon-yellow t-shirts embroidered with *"Wendy's Weirdos."* Then I got a matching shirt for me that simply said, *"Wendy."*

Late that night, my mom dropped me off at camp. I ran to our bunk and turned on the light. One-by-one, the girls sat up, groaning, rubbing their eyes and uttering words they'd never have used with their parents.

"Get up," I beamed, *"I have a gift for you!"*

They loved the shirts! Score one for the counselor.

While they put on their shirts, I invited them to join me for a *"secret meeting of Wendy's Weirdos"* at the lake.

"Now?!" They asked. *"Won't we get in trouble?"*

"Since when do you care about that?" I smiled. *"Come on, let's go!"*

Giddy and giggling, we tiptoed out of the building, shushing each other as we scurried down to the lake. It was chilly, so we bundled up beneath blankets and I announced the official launch of the Wendy's Weirdos Club, *"Wendy's Weirdos is an exclusive group of young women who are unique and brilliant and so incredibly special."* To my surprise, I got choked up as I said it.

I wish you could've seen the looks on their faces. Suddenly these scary monsters morphed into round little cherubs who looked about three years old.

We sat under the full moon, sang a few songs and talked about all the ways they saw themselves as *different.* I had hoped this would bring them closer but I never imagined how powerful it would be for them—and for me. We shared a night of sacred conversations as they revealed intimate stories about being teased and ostracized at school, left out from social activities and constantly criticized for their appearance. Many expressed anger at their parents for shaming them into coming to "fat camp."

One-by-one, they transformed from unmanageable, self-involved kids to a cohesive team of young women who shared a bond of humiliation and membership in a "secret society" where they finally belonged.

Empowered by the knowledge they weren't alone, the rest of the summer was magical as they clung tightly to each other and discovered the joy of friendship—for the first time in their lives. Every Wednesday was "Weirdo Day" and we wore our t-shirts proudly through the camp.

At the end of the summer, my young women had lost more total pounds than any in the camp and there were tears and hugs all around as we said goodbye.

Significant transformation occurs when you use the power of ethical influence to move people to action.

After that summer I devoted myself to finding the full set of factors that move people to action. In college, graduate school and beyond I studied sociology, social psychology, neuropsychology, anthropology, biology, clinical psychology and organizational psychology, searching for all the pieces to the puzzle of what makes us do what we do. Finally, I compiled what I call, the **Science of Impact**™ and it was time to test it in the "real" world.

Over the next 20 years, I developed, tested, refined, retested and ultimately discovered 18 sets of formulas that consistently and ethically influence people so you can maximize and capitalize on your impact. I used *the Move People to Action System for Experts, Executives and Entrepreneurs*™ to help my clients get extraordinary results in every industry from manufacturers to make-up artists, and I use it to this day.

I'd love to teach the complete system to you now but that would distract you from the steps you need to get complete clarity on the rest of your Focus On Impact Map. Instead, I'm going to teach you three formulas you can use right away to deliver your impact with measurable results and then give you a gift to access the rest of my formulas at your convenience.[62]

FORMULA # 1: CAPITALIZE ON THE 7 CRITICAL ACTIONS

Of the many actions people take in life, there are only seven that are critical to your success in business. Move people to take these actions in order and you will consistently maximize and monetize your impact.

Action # 1: Find You

When people have a problem, there is a critical window between the moment they *perceive* a problem and the moment they take action to *solve* the problem. Sometimes that action can take a long time. (Ever cut a coupon out of a newspaper and put it on your refrigerator, only to find it months later?)

You need to be right there at that *final-straw* moment, and move them to action so they experience the results of your impact and accelerate their transition between pain and action.

Use your Impact Platform Power to help people find you, and use the C.O.N.T.E.N.T. Formula[63] to move people to action!

Once they've experienced your impact, their next critical action will be to…

Action # 2: Follow You

Your *60 Weeks of Impact* will give you ongoing opportunities to address every challenge being faced by your Table For 12 market. When you sequence your impact effectively, people will be driven to make sure

---

62   To access your gift, see Page 185.
63   See Chapter 8.

they get all your Impact Gifts. The more people follow you, the more the algorithms will kick in, growing your reach and your impact exponentially. Over time, you'll be addressing all the results they need in order to be ready to buy your products/services. But before they'll be willing to buy from you, you've got to move them to…

Action # 3: Choose You

There is nothing more humbling than when people choose you to help them in their businesses and/or personal lives. A sacred trust is formed between you that's unlike any outside your family or closest friends. Choosing you as their go-to resource for information and/or entertainment is a huge compliment and tribute to the wonderful work you've done to impact their lives. It also sets up an unbreakable connection that helps them feel comfortable coming to you for more.

Never underestimate the value of someone opening and reading your email, watching your video, listening to your podcast, attending your webinar, commenting on your blog or inviting you to speak to, or write for, their audience.

People have a lot of choices out there, so when they choose you, that says a lot. Remember to thank them, connect with them and let them know you see them as real people, with real lives, real pain and real dreams. Let them know you're happy to see them and help them feel welcome in your business, your community and your life.

Do that well, and they'll be ready to take the next critical action…

Action # 4: Buy From You

Please take a moment and notice buying is Action # 4 out of the seven. The simple truth is out of everything you'll do, getting them to buy will be the easiest!

The hard part is helping them conquer change resistance so they'll easily make a series of decisions to want more than you've given them week after week in your impact-driven marketing.

Don't worry about getting people to buy.
Focus on what comes before and after they buy.

When you move people to action so they implement the tips you give in your Impact Gifts, they become increasingly aware that something is missing in their lives. This capitalizes on a very cool principle in sociology called *relative deprivation*.

I was perfectly fine with what I had until you showed me what I could have. Now I want that.

The moment people become aware that something's missing, there's a shift. Sometimes the shift increases excitement and a desire to own. At other times, it leads to a sense of fear, vulnerability and even embarrassment.

Before we buy anything, we have to admit (if only to
ourselves) there is something we're missing that we
can't (or don't want to) live without.
This creates a dilemma because many people
would rather live without than admit they need/want
something they don't have.

The more personal your products/services, the more you need to understand how to help people get through this dilemma.

Example: You're at the drug store waiting to pay for an item that will relieve a personal problem you don't want anyone to know you've got. The line is incredibly long and, of course, your neighbor comes in and sees you standing there.

Luckily, the line moves and it's your turn to go to the register (phew!). The cashier picks up the item and can't find the price. Now he holds it up high and yells over the noise to his colleague across the store, announcing the name of the item and waving it through the air to be sure he sees it.

GRRRRRRRR.

You leave the item on the counter, walk quickly to the nearest exit and go next door to the grocery store to buy a pint of ice cream.

You go to the first check out aisle and the cashier looks vaguely familiar. As you hand her the ice cream you lock eyes and suddenly you remember! She was in the free seminar you gave yesterday called, *"Dairy: The Hidden Problem."*

UGH.

Oh! I left my wallet in the car. And off you go, making a mental note not to shop there again.

That night you're sitting at your desk, scraping the remaining ice cream off the bottom of a container you found in your freezer. Just as you complete your purchase of an online course on how to manage your bookkeeping, your spouse walks in and says,

"Maybe you should be concentrating on MAKING money before you worry about how to keep track of it. How much did you spend on that anyway?"

You scroll down to cancel your order. In the "Reason for Cancelling" box, you type, *"Don't need it."*

No matter what your product or service, at some point it's likely that someone is going to hesitate or even walk away. Always remember:

A consumer's job is to say no, if only to prove
s/he doesn't need your products/services.

The simpler your buying process, and the more you use Formula # 3,[64] the more likely people will buy. But even when they buy, you've got another huge hurdle to jump…

Action # 5: Use What They Buy

I conducted a research study of 3000 entrepreneurs who had attended business development seminars. Among many of the items we covered, a fascinating statistic appeared:

---

64 See Page 112

100% of respondents reported they had purchased a business development product, paying up to $1000, but hadn't read, watched or listened to what they'd bought.

What about you? Have you ever purchased a book but never read it? Ordered a product but haven't opened it? How about a gym membership that somehow got forgotten? Or a garment that still has the tags attached? Or my all-time favorite: Do you own an expensive exercise machine but only use it to hang wet towels?

We all buy things we don't use. The question is WHY?

The simple answer is, we lose interest. The complex answer is, whatever moved us to *buy* wasn't enough to move us to *use*. Either way, the end result is *buyer's remorse* and *stuff-it-in-the-closet* syndrome.

What will you do to move people to action so they will be driven to use what they buy and get measurable results from your impact?

The secret is to infuse comments, questions and tips throughout your *60 Weeks of Impact* that will invite people to visualize and experience how life could be different after they get the results you can deliver. Do that well and the decisions to buy AND use will be automatic.

Of course, the most important thing you can do is develop your one-of-a-kind products/services so they make the impact you promised! The more results people achieve from using your products/services, the less likely you'll have to do anything at all to move them to the next action...

Action # 6: Tell Their Friends

People tell their friends about a product/service when it is memorable and the memories are either great or awful, but not in between. So the first step is to commit to creating wonderful memories from the first moment of contact through the life of your product/service and well beyond. That will happen when you Sequence Your Impact with one-of-a-kind products and services and send out impact-driven marketing year round.

Take charge of people's memories by deciding what you want your buyers to remember about their experiences with you, your team, and your products/services. Then determine what you'll do to help their memories be so outstanding, they can't help but think and talk about you! That will happen naturally when your impact leads to measurable results.

When you deliver your products/services to move people to action, their results will be measurable, memorable and noticeable by others.

The ultimate goal is to develop and deliver your products/services so the impact will be readily noticed by your consumers' friends without prompting.

"Wow! You seem different! What have you been doing?"

"Oh! I started working with a new coach. She's amazing!"

"Well I just can't get over the change in you. What's your coach's name?"

Score!

Action # 7 Come Back for More

It's much easier (and way less expensive) to serve a repeat customer than to entice someone you've never met. The great news is when you use the strategies I gave you to Sequence Your Impact[65] and combine that with the formulas I'm about to teach you to move people to action, your buyers will get measurable results and naturally be driven to come back for more—over and over and over again. Not only is that good for your business, it's good for your soul. It tells you you're doing a lot of things right.

Over the course of my career, a significantly high percentage of my clients have purchased more than one product or service. It's a

---

65   See Chapter 7.

tremendous honor when clients come back for more—particularly when I get to see how much progress they've made since we last met.

I especially love it when alumni keep coming back to my *Move People to Action Live Events*. This is a 4-day, comprehensive training, and yet they come back—some as many as *seven* times! Why would someone invest the time and money to come back more than once—let alone seven times?

I've asked my alumni what drives them to keep coming back and while their answers include a wide variety of reasons, there is one thing they all have in common,

"I learn something new every time."

That's not luck—it's strategy. I do what I've taught you to do: I sequence the impact of my training so when people go home and implement what they learned, they get results that lead to immediate and permanent changes in how they think, what they do, what they feel and what they get. When they come back the next time, they're in a different stage of development so they actually hear, see and feel things they weren't *ready* to hear, see or feel before.

Starbucks˙ is another great example of getting people to come back for more. Once you've had your first cup of coffee, you're in a different state of mind and body than you were before that cup. Now you're ready for something else. How about a specialty coffee? Or a cold bottle of water? Hungry? Maybe a banana or something sweet? Even if you don't want something more today, you'll be coming back for more tomorrow. Because the feeling you get from your Starbucks experience is consistent, and because it doesn't last. So if you want that feeling, you've got to come back for more.

Of course, Apple is the master of Action # 7. Once you've experienced an Apple product, you've just got to come back for the next thing or to get a second thing as backup in case your first thing goes down or to grab an accessory to make your first thing better, faster, easier or cooler or just to play with things you're not yet ready to buy. Need I say more?

The point is that if you effectively move people to action in Actions 1–6, Action # 7 will be automatic.

Cool! What else ya got?

I'm so glad you asked! Thanks for coming back for more! Let's look at another of my favorite Move People to Action formulas:

FORMULA # 2: THE RULE OF 5

When I opened my first brick-and-mortar business, I had no idea what the "rules" of business were or how to make it all turn out okay. I'd opened *East of Eden* on a whim after managing a stressful research project that had landed me at the U.S. Senate with a tremendous amount riding on the report I delivered there.

It all came to a head when I shared a bottle of wine with a friend who happened to be my hair stylist. I rarely drank, so after two glasses I was on another planet. I shared the stress of my job and she talked about her horrible boss. We laughed and laughed and one thing led to the next and suddenly we were discussing how wonderful it would be to launch our own business.

I grabbed a paper napkin and started to sketch an elaborate styling salon and spa. I knew absolutely nothing about the beauty business but she was a hair stylist and we had fun imagining what we'd do there. I stayed up all night elaborating on the plan and the next morning I walked into a bank with my napkin sketch and a proposal to build a Full-Service Styling Salon/Spa that would be a social laboratory to test formulas to move people to action.

I was a credible candidate, and loans were much easier to come by back then. They gave me $50,000 and I spent it all building a magnificent shop equipped with plants and birds and everything else I could think of to create a modern-day Garden of Eden in the middle of Fort Worth, TX. My friend had no interest in any of it now that the wine had worn off, so I quit my job at the university and went off to launch my adventure.

Understand, I had no idea how to build a business or get customers (which worked out well since I didn't have any stylists). My expenses were astronomical but I was determined to make it work. Long story short, in 6 months I had 12 operators and we were breaking records for retail sales.

It all accelerated when one of my customers said, *"I need one lipstick for work and another for evenings."*

WOW! That woman was living two lives! Were there more lives she wasn't telling me about? What about my other customers? I decided to find out and launched a study to discover how many lives the women in my market were living. As it turned out, there were five:

- ✓ Home (alone or with family).
- ✓ Work (or any occasion when scrutinized by people in a position of power/authority)
- ✓ Play (exercise, casual sporting or fun with friends)
- ✓ Evening Social (cocktail parties, romantic or special occasion dinners)
- ✓ High Profile Celebrations (New Years, Weddings, Awards banquets)

I ran an ad in the local newspaper in which I asked one question and gave one easy answer:

How many faces should you wear? One for every woman you are!

The results: In one week our retail sales grew from less than $1000 per week to $5000[66] (the growth continued over time as I discovered more powerful formulas).

That was 30 years ago, and since then I've found the *Rule of 5* holds true across multiple industries, online and off.

The Rule of 5:
Help people connect the benefits of your products/services with 5 unique areas of their lives!

---

66   $5000 in 1983 converts to $11,853.36US, $14,432.90CA or €10,897.20 in 2015.

How Many Faces Should You Wear?*

Rose Ross
Cosmetics
and
Skin Care

Available
Exclusively
at
East
of
Eden

*One for every woman you are!

Finding the right make-up for your individual needs is as personal as choosing your wardrobe. (You wouldn't wear an evening gown to breakfast, why wear your breakfast face to the theatre?)

Whether the occasion calls for a light touch of blush or a dazzling display of colors, your trained Rose Ross consultant will help you find that special look which best suits your individual lifestyle. She'll show you how to use Rose Ross cosmetics and skin care to help your skin realize its own radiant potential.

today for your personal consultation and free, customized make-over.

3009 Lackland Road   738-9530

*Your one-stop oasis
for total personalized care.*

Use the Rule of 5 to deliver your impact and move people to action by helping your market imagine multiple uses and benefits of your products and services. Show them how different areas of their lives will be impacted—not by *buying* what you offer, but by *using* what they buy. And show them how to use it in all five areas of their lives!

Then you'll be ready to conquer change resistance...

FORMULA # 3: THE ACTION FORMULA

In Chapter 3, I invited you to define your impact and then use the Action Formula so you'd have sufficient DESIRE, RESOURCES and PERMISSION to make it happen.

Now come with me behind the curtains of my own business so I can reveal for you another power of the Action Formula.

Step back in time and remember what originally moved you to pick up this book and bring it into your life. Once you owned this book, what moved you to open and read it? What's *keeping* you reading it?

What is moving you to *use* the advice I'm giving you here, to *do* the Action Steps and ultimately what will move you to *use* the complete Focus on Impact Map to reach millions, make millions and love your life along the way?[67]

Whatever your answers to those questions, the bottom line is you're moving *yourself* to action in response to what I'm doing here. And what I'm doing is USING the Action Formula at every step of my service to you.

From designing the cover of this book to choosing the words on each page...every comma, every italicized word or phrase, every graphic, every online resource, everything was purposefully chosen and consciously placed to address one or more of the three components in your Action Formula.

Why do I work so hard at this?

---

67 If you haven't yet completed Action Step # 1, please do that now. Then go on to the next and the next. These Action Steps are critical to your ability to capitalize on this book.

My mission is to make a lasting impact on your life so you, in turn, will go out and make an impact on every life you touch.

To make that happen, I need to move you to action, so you'll move yourself to action. Otherwise, you might not capture the dreams that led you to pick up this book—and that's not an option. The world needs your impact, so I use the Action Formula to help you grow your DESIRE so you'll never lose momentum on the way to making your greatest impact and reaping the rewards of your difference.

I use the Action Formula to choose which formulas I teach you, which stories I tell, which downloadable pieces I have for you at FocusOnImpact.com/resources and on our Online Community page and which parting gifts I'll give you when you're done reading. All of these items are the RESOURCES I'm bringing you so you'll have a greater ability to achieve your DESIRES.

Lastly, I use the Action Formula to provide all the insights you need so you'll give yourself PERMISSION to use the Focus On Impact Map and be WILLING to finally let yourself have everything you so richly deserve.

You have given me the privilege of helping you capture your dreams and I hold your trust sacred. That's why I'm using the Action Formula so I can deliver my impact and move you to action. I'm inviting you to do the same for the people you serve (and for all you hope to serve).

You see, your ultimate challenge when you Focus On Impact is this:

People stop themselves from letting themselves have what they truly want.

Your most important job is to help people identify and hold onto their DESIRE in your marketing[68] and long after they buy. Remember to infuse your marketing with reminders of how their lives will be

---

68   When you differentiate with impact-driven content marketing, the
C.O.N.T.E.N.T. Formula will help you!

improved as a result of using your products and services and help them know they deserve to have that better life. Keep going long after they buy so they'll be excited to use everything you give them, and so they'll continue to see you as their go-to RESOURCE. Then help them give themselves PERMISSION to take action, use what they buy and come back for more.

Use the Action Formula in every city on your Focus On Impact Map!

The more you deliver your impact to move people to action, the more your influence and impact will grow, the more people will buy and the more money you'll make. And that's a really good thing. Because the more money you make, the faster you'll be able to take your mind off of money and place your Focus On Impact.

And when you Focus On Impact, even more money will come!

Are there more formulas you can use to deliver your impact and move people to action? Yes, but the most important thing you can do right now is get comfortable using the three formulas I've given you here. Start now with Action Step # 9. Then we'll move on to maximize your impact in the City of DIVERSIFY.

ACTION STEP #9

Deliver Your Impact And Move People To Action!

Now you're ready to really make things happen – for the people you serve, for your team, for your family and for YOU! It's time to enhance everything we've done so far with the three formulas I've given you to deliver your impact and move people to action. Here's how:

First, look at the 6 products/services you mapped out in the City of DEVELOP. For each product/service on your list, decide how you'll move people to take the 7 Critical Actions.

Hint: When you infuse the Action Formula into each product/service you create, you'll get significantly more people to use what they buy, tell their friends and come back for more.

Next, capitalize on the Rule of 5 by developing one question you will send to your Table for 12 market to get them thinking about how they would use your products/services across their five lives.

Finally, go to your *60 Weeks of Impact Planning Sheet* and make sure you're using the C.O.N.T.E.N.T. Formula in each impact-driven content piece you create.

Hint: If you go too long without taking these three steps, go back to Chapter 3 and review your Action Formula so you move yourself to action!

The next step is to create an even bigger impact in the City of DIVERSIFY!

The world is waiting for your impact. Turn the page for City # 8 of your Focus On Impact Map!

Chapter Ten

DIVERSIFY
WITH IMPACT-DRIVEN
COLLABORATION

*The impact we make together will be far greater
than any we can ever make alone.*

hat do the following items have in common?

Green Smoothie ◆ Symphony Orchestra ◆ Birthday Cake
◆ Teaching Hospital ◆ Brick House ◆ Purple Crayon ◆
Married Couple

The answer: these entities exist only because two or more stand-alone products and/or people came together. The result was a greater impact than they could have ever made alone.

Impact-Driven Collaboration™ is the process of bringing together two or more companies for the purpose of developing and delivering a new product or service that creates an impact far stronger than either company could have created alone. This method of diversification is the most powerful, cost-effective business accelerator I've ever found.

Why is diversification so important to growing your impact? Because no matter how amazing your products/services may be, your current offerings will never be enough to meet all the needs of the people you serve. You can stick with what you know and refer your customers/clients/patients/donors on to others, *or* you can grow your impact exponentially through collaboration.

Impact-Driven Collaborative Partnerships enable you to serve more people than you could ever reach alone with new products and services that yield synergistic results—for you, your partner(s) and your combined markets!

I first discovered Impact-Driven Collaboration in 1982 when I was managing a massive research project at a university. Our little team was making great progress, but I kept thinking there was something we were missing. I needed an out-of-the-box idea that would allow us to go deeper and find a truth we couldn't see.

I sent letters to doctors and researchers around the globe, inviting them to attend a summit for the purpose of combining their wisdom and experience to find a new research instrument that would enable us to find more answers for our client hospital. To my surprise, all invitees accepted and when they arrived, it was more than a little daunting.

Everyone who attended was much older and more experienced than I, yet since I was project manager, it was up to me to facilitate the day. As I watched them arrive, I wondered how I would be able to get them to put their egos aside and work together to find one solution.

Collaboration begins with mutually agreed-upon guidelines that honor the expertise of everyone involved.

I presented guidelines and then I asked a single question in hopes of unlocking the vault of their collaborative genius:

What can we create together here in this room that will generate a greater impact than any one of us could ever make alone?

My question sparked an energetic exchange that escalated beyond anything I'd ever experienced. Ideas were flying around the room so quickly I couldn't get them on the chalkboard. There was nothing left for me to do but marvel at the avalanche of brilliance that bounced off the walls and rattled the windows.

The conversations went on for hours and then suddenly, silence filled the room. Without being told, we all knew we'd found the answer, although no one was sure who had originated the concept. Not one person tried to claim the discovery because no one was sure who'd said it first. The answer simply appeared as if by magic, but we all knew it was very real—the natural result of complete immersion in a single problem and an unwavering Focus On Impact.

These austere grown-ups spontaneously broke into fits of laughter with wild applause, back-slapping hugs, and tears flowing freely from their excited eyes.

There's nothing like the feeling that hits you the moment you realize the magnitude of the impact you're about to make on people's lives.

That night I made a silent vow to build my skills and influence so that someday I could create a massive collaboration with a more diversified array of difference-makers from around the globe. My fantasy was I'd facilitate their collaboration for the purpose of developing new solutions for all the problems we face on our planet. It was a big dream, but I was determined to make it happen.

Since then, I've had the privilege of facilitating hundreds of collaborations, helping my clients come together with people they'd considered competition to create impact-driven collaborative projects, increase their diversity and achieve greater results—for the people they serve and themselves.

I launched a movement to attract impact-driven men and women from around the globe and welcomed them into my Community of Difference-Makers™ so they could support each other to Focus On Impact and make connections for collaborative projects.

I built my own impact-driven collaborations, resulting in powerful products that brought a synergistic impact to our mutual markets, lasting friendships among my partners and significant rewards for everyone involved.

Then in July, 2015, I finally captured my 35-year dream when experts, executives, entrepreneurs, educators, employees and entertainers from around the globe accepted my invitation to join me for the world's first, *Difference-Maker Summit*™ and *Global Collaboration Project*™—this is what happens when you Focus On Impact. Dreams come true and the result is extraordinary.[69]

Imagine what would happen if entrepreneurs, entertainers, educators, small business owners, corporate executives, non-profit leaders, doctors, credentialed professionals and all employees, staff and volunteers came together in small groups once per year for the purpose of finding impact-driven, collaborative solutions for the problems in the world. The results would be extraordinary—beyond anything we can imagine.

Your ideal collaborative partners will inspire new creativity in you, as you will in them. To make it happen, get clarity on your impact and then follow these 12 steps:

12 STEPS FOR IMPACT-DRIVEN COLLABORATION THAT SUCCEEDS!

Step 1: Protect Your Impact

If collaboration is new to you, check with an attorney for assistance in protecting your intellectual property before entering into any conversations about your business.[70]

---

69 See Page 187 for discounted access to the next Difference-Maker Summit.
70 To meet some of my favorite IP attorneys, visit FocusOnImpact.com/resources

Step 2: Research Your Missing Pieces

Research your market to identify and fully understand their problems. Follow social discussions to learn how those problems are affecting their lives and keep a watchful eye for issues that go beyond your capabilities so you'll know what to look for in your future partnerships.

Next, use the Collaboration Chart on Page 121 and place an "X" next to each area you are equipped to address for your market.

Now go back over the chart again and place an "O" next to each market need that you don't meet.

VOILÀ! You're ready to find your collaborative partners!

Step 3: Build Relationships with Potential Partners

Seek out people who provide solutions for the needs you can't serve. Do your due diligence and when you find a good fit, start a conversation that begins with:

We have similar markets and while our products and services are different, we both address key needs the other doesn't touch. Let's have a conversation to explore what we might do together that would make an impact far greater than either one of us will ever make alone.

Remember, the ultimate goal is to create impact-driven, collaborative solutions that address all the pain reported by your market. So always be on the lookout for potential partners who can fill your gaps.

Step 4: Find Compatible Products/Services

It's critical your future partners' offerings fit with, and enhance yours. Let's say you are a plastic surgeon. Your research reveals your market often comments about wardrobe problems. The obvious collaborative partners would be image experts, tailors and local clothing stores, along with a fitness expert and nutritionist to help maintain and enhance your interventions. Together you might create an Image Fair where you'd

IMPACT-DRIVEN COLLABORATION

Impact	X	O	Impact	X	O	Impact	X	O
Motivation			Small Business			Alcoholism/Drugs		
Leadership			Sales			Battling Cancer		
Education/ Teaching			Human Resources			Internet marketing		
Faith & Religion			Technology			Relationships		
New Media			Arts/Culture/Music			Productivity		
Lifestyle			Entertainment			Military life		
Sports			Health & Wellness			Inspiration		
Politics			History			Strategic Planning		
Creative Arts			Music Production			Music Teaching		
Family			Parenting			Stress		
Women's issues			Men's issues			Writing/publishing		
Self-help			Career Planning			Aging / Anti-Aging		
Conflict			Life Balance			Retirement		
Bereavement			Real Estate			Engineering		
Diversity			Domestic Violence			Children's stories		
Public Relations			Adventures			Fitness		
Medical/Dental			Negotiation			Photography		
Pets/Animals			Image Mgmt			Organization		
Productivity			Web Development			Wellness		
Spirituality			Graphic Design			Ghost Writing		
Publishing			Copywriting			Legal Services		
Social Media			Traditional Media			Nutrition		
Branding			Virtual Assistance			Non-Profit		
Raising Capital			Crowd Funding			Sponsorship		
Video Production			Online Advertising			Networking		
Personnel Selection			Product Design			Retail Marketing		
Sales and Marketing			Psychology			Interior Design		
Financial/ Accounting			Multi-Level Marketing			Time management		

invite your shared markets to enjoy an afternoon of fun, education and sampling. Ultimately, you could come together to create a Lifetime-Healthy-Image Program that included all your services.

If you're in the business of giving how-to advice, the key to your collaboration will be to find partners who offer advice that fills in your missing gaps. For example, if you're a business consultant, look at time management, goal achievement and personal development experts so you have every area covered.

Remember: the goal is to bring everyone together to create one product/service that addresses multiple market needs.

Step 5: Check Ethical Congruence

Share the ethical pillars of your business and ask them to do the same. If your would-be partner isn't immediately ready to respond, don't panic. It may be he or she hasn't given this a lot of thought, but still holds values that fit with yours. Probe until you're clear there is congruence in your business ethics.

Step 6: Assure Equality

Impact-driven collaboration works best when there are equal stakes, equal resources and equal rewards. Establish expectations of equality up front and put everything in writing. Without clear equality expectations, you will never be willing to play full out. Remember:

Don't assume equality, document it.

Step 7: Place Impact above Self

Collaboration only works when ego-driven spotlights are dimmed in the interest of shining a light on your combined impact. Make sure your collaborative packaging spotlights everyone fairly so you can Focus On Impact and everyone wins.

Step 8: Establish Accountability

Far too many collaborations never see completion because one or more partners fail to live up to their commitment to the project. It's critically important that you outline responsibilities, expectations, deadlines, rewards, sanctions and acceptable exceptions in advance so everyone is clear from the beginning.

Step 9: Get Someone to Facilitate

In the ideal scenario, all partners will be free to maintain focus on the project whenever you come together for meetings (in person or virtually). In order to make that happen, get a facilitator to lead your sessions, ask guiding questions, and hold everyone accountable to agreements and expectations. Even if budget isn't available for this, find someone everyone can agree upon to serve as your third-party facilitator in exchange for project benefits.

Step 10: Define Your Collaborative Impact

Work to get complete clarity on the unique impact you can make together. Your first step will be to outline the measurable results you want to bring to your combined markets.

Never start a project without clarity of your outcomes.

Step 11: Develop Your One-of-a-Kind Product/Service

The new collaborative products and services you create must align with your Impact Action Formula[71] and your Ideal Lifestyle Design.[72] Invite your partner(s) to discuss their impact and lifestyle goals and create your new product/service to suit everyone involved (including your combined market). You'll be much more likely to take this to completion if all partners are excited about the process of developing and delivering your one-of-a-kind collaboration.

---

71 See Chapter 3.
72 See Chapter 5.

Step 12: Differentiate with Collaborative Impact-Driven Marketing

Everything grows exponentially the moment you pull together your mutual resources to get this message out to the world. All the strategies are the same as described in Chapter 8, but the fun really begins when you create collaborative C.O.N.T.E.N.T. pieces to send out to your combined markets in a collaborative promotion that is crafted by both of you to combine your messages and fly. #impact #income #celebrate

WILL YOU SUCCEED?

Once you achieve complete clarity on your unique Focus On Impact Map and then follow the 12 Steps for Impact-Driven Collaboration above, every collaborative partnership will be an experience you'll cherish. Each new project will build your skills, make a greater impact, grow your reach further and build your revenues. The more projects you create, the faster you'll find the perfect formula for you. In the meantime, you'll reap rewards you can't yet imagine as you connect with other impact-driven people.

Here's a quick story from my own path that may inspire you to take a risk and see where it leads you…

In 1998 I discovered an ever-increasing percentage of my corporate audiences was filled with women who appeared tired, agitated and more than a little stressed. After some research, I discovered it was worse than I'd thought. Well over 80% of women between the ages of 38 and 55 reported multiple physical and psychological symptoms that were keeping them from being effective at work and at home.

I was driven to help them, and I knew teaching stress management and business skills simply weren't going to be enough. I decided to seek advice from an expert I'd known for 13 years who had an unusually comprehensive background. He had medical school training, a PhD in counseling psychology (trained in nine different schools of psychology), was triple-board certified in psychoanalysis, and had a second PhD in environmental medicine. He'd been in private practice for 25 years, was the go-to resource for physicians in his community and was a consulting psychologist for multi-national corporations. I had no doubt he'd have valuable information to share about the problems I was seeing.

I flew 2000 miles to take him to lunch, and in the middle of my salad I got a great idea:

Let's combine our knowledge and offer a series of seminars to teach women about the psychological, social psychological, medical, neuropsychological, environmental and business-related causes of their symptoms, and show them how to take charge of all of it!

He loved the idea. We worked out a plan to get past the 2000-mile distance between us by working during the week by phone and face-to-face on available weekends. We flew back and forth for a few months and the result was a seminar unlike anything that had ever been offered worldwide. I developed a powerful marketing campaign, signed contracts for four events at a high-end venue and we both blocked our calendars. It was an expensive, risky venture but we were determined to get this information out to the women who needed it.

Over the next four months, we had the privilege of helping wonderful women get their lives back and had a fabulous time doing it! And while the meeting rooms were never as fully packed as we would have liked, we both agreed it was well worth our time. We learned a lot from each other, made a bigger impact than we could have ever made alone, and on top of all of that, we fell in love!

Since then, Dr. Hal Dibner and I have collaborated on hundreds of projects that brought measurable results for the people we served—and for our family. Every day I'm grateful for the decision we both made over lunch that led to opportunities beyond anything either of us had imagined possible.[73]

Today we continue to run our separate businesses, and frequently collaborate on special projects. And on those occasions, I get to serve with an expert I deeply respect who happens to be the love of my life.

You never know where an impact-driven collaboration will lead you.

---

73 Meet my amazing husband at FocusOnImpact.com/resources

Start planning now so you can diversify with impact-driven collaborations. Begin with Action Step # 10 and then I'll show you how to make great decisions for your business in the City of DECIDE.

ACTION STEP #10

Diversify with Impact-Driven Collaboration

Are you excited to increase your impact, your reach and your revenues exponentially?

First, make a decision to forget about competition and move into the cooperative model of impact-driven collaborative partnerships.

Next, follow Steps 1 – 12 above and create your synergistic impact!

Once you've experienced the power of this approach, do it again with a new group of partners and develop another collaborative product/service.

Remember – the impact you make together will be far greater than any you'll ever create alone.

The next step is to protect and expand your impact further in the City of DECIDE! [74]

The world is waiting for your impact. Turn the page for City # 9 of your Focus On Impact Map!

---

[74] To understand more fully the power of cooperation in business, read *Redemption: The Cooperative Revolution* by Berny Dohrmann.

Chapter Eleven

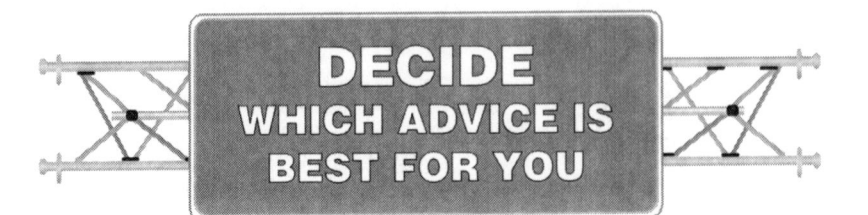

DECIDE
WHICH ADVICE IS
BEST FOR YOU

Any business model can be used to grow a business,
but not every business model is right for you.

A treasured client once confided, *"I've spent over $300,000 to get business advice. Some of it was good, a lot of it wasn't. But I just take some of each thing. You know—a little bit o' this, a little bit o' that."*

"So how's that working for you?" I asked.

"It's not!" she laughed.

Open your inbox and you'll find a tsunami of emails filled with people offering you advice to grow your business. Try to watch a video online or read an article and you'll wait as much as 17 seconds before you can *Skip the Ad*. Attend a multi-speaker conference and get flooded with conflicting advice that leads you to break your *After-5 Rule* before lunch!

The greater your impact, the more advice will come your way.

That's really good news because it's impossible to know what lies ahead on a path you've never traveled. It's critical to have people in your life who can show you the curves, detours, road blocks and hazards that could keep you from maximizing and capitalizing on your unique impact.

You need experts who will give you advice. But here's the killer question:

Who knows what's best for YOU? [75]

The biggest mistakes in my life have always fallen into one of two categories:

1. I neglected to seek help when I didn't know how to do something, or

2. I went against my instincts.

The answer: Only you know what's best for you.

Okay, yeah—I know, but how can I be sure that what I think is best is really best? He's done so much more than I have; she's a bestselling author; he has years of experience over me; she's bringing in eight figures a year!

Here's what I've discovered in my own career, and let's see if it makes sense for you:

Just because someone has accomplished something more—or different—than you, it doesn't mean that person knows what's best for you.

Here are **5 Steps to Decide Which Advice is Best For You:**

---

75 I'm very aware of how weird it is that I'm about to give you advice in a chapter about how to decide which advice is best for you. I guess the first "decision" you'll need to make is whether to take my advice on how to decide which advice is best for you! How's that for a mind twister? ☺ Seriously, I'm deeply honored you're reading this and hope you will find this helpful.

STEP 1: LOOK INWARD

The human brain is a finely tuned instrument that detects signals that are out of our conscious awareness. While it often takes hours (or even years) to find words to describe what the brain has figured out, the brain has another way to communicate: through feelings.

**"Your feelings tell you one of two things:
There's either a pleasure to be enjoyed or a problem to be solved."
— Hal Dibner, PhD**

Have you ever felt a fast bolt of energy rip through your body when a car cuts you off in traffic? That surge alerts you to a present danger so you can act quickly without having to find words to figure out you're in trouble.

There is also another sensation you get when you melt into the world's most comfortable couch next to someone you love. That feeling is present when we're safe and happy.

In addition to physical sensations, we've got a host of emotions that come into play. These feelings carry many messages for us to hear and interpret, though it's not always black and white. You may not know *what* is upsetting you, so it's important to recognize that you're upset and trace it to the point where you can identify the source. Your job is to discover what your brain is trying to tell you.

I'm really irritable but I have no idea what I'm mad about!

Is something happening you don't like?

No.

Did someone say or do something you didn't like or not do something you wanted?

No.

When's the last time you ate something?

Uh…I don't remember. Maybe around six this morning.

It's 6:30 p.m.

Hmm. That would explain it. I just got caught up in work and lost track of time. Maybe I should eat something.

When you pay attention to the signals from your brain, you will discover an extraordinarily powerful tool that is completely at your command. Not only will this tool help you take better care of yourself and those around you, it will also tell you precisely which advice is right for you, which is questionable, and which is a big mistake.

If you take no other piece of advice in this entire book, please take this:

When someone offers you advice, trust your instincts.

When I learned that, my entire world shifted.

STEP 2: FIND YOUR FIT

By design, the Focus On Impact Map is a tool you can use to assess whether any piece of advice is a good fit for you. Whenever you get advice like, *Buy my X,* go immediately to your Map and determine which city the advice best serves.

Next, look at what you've accomplished to date in that city. Are you where you want to be or is something still missing?

If you're where you want to be, the best advice for you will be something that will either (1) sustain your current status or (2) improve your status in one or more additional cities you haven't taken into account.

If you're not where you want to be, there are two questions to be addressed:

(1) How could this advice help me?

To find the answer, run through your Focus On Impact Map:

✓ **DEFINE:** Will it help you get clarity on your unique IMPACT and Ethical Pillars? Will it help you fill in a gap that's missing on your RESOURCE list? Will it bring

you more PERMISSION? Will it take you closer to your
DESIREs?

✓ **DISCOVER:** Will it help you identify and capitalize on all
your unique gifts?

✓ **DESIGN:** Does it fit your UPtime, DOWNtime and MEtime
parameters?

✓ **DETERMINE:** Does it fit your unique Table For 12 Market?

✓ **DEVELOP:** Will it help you discover or create one-of-a-kind
products and services?

✓ **DIFFERENTIATE:** Will it get your message out further and
faster by capitalizing on your Impact-Driven Content? Will it
give you more Impact Platform Power?

✓ **DELIVER:** Will it help you deliver your impact by moving
people to action?

✓ **DIVERSIFY:** Will it bring you more diversity through
impact-driven collaborations?

✓ **DECIDE:** Will it help you know which advice is best for you?

✓ **DARE:** Will it help you grow bigger?

If the advice doesn't fit anywhere on your map, it's probably not
right for you—at least not yet. File it in your "Shiny Objects" folder.

*(2) If this advice fits into my Map, is the person/company offering the
advice right for me?*

For that answer, you'll need to do two things: First, check your
instincts. What do you feel in your body when you think about the
person or company giving you that advice? Scared? Excited? Mad? Calm?
Depressed? Proud? Embarrassed? Happy? Guilty? Tired? Energized?
Ashamed? Relieved? All of the above?

**If you like how you feel in response to the
person/company, that's a good sign!**

But before you make a firm decision, consider Step 3…

STEP 3: SEEK ADDITIONAL PERSPECTIVE

Sometimes a decision is hard because we're missing data. When you're missing information, you'll have a skewed perspective, so contact people you trust and ask the right questions. The best sources are:

(1) Team members, close family, customers and anyone who would be directly affected by your decision to take the advice. Here is language you can use to begin the conversation:

*I'm considering taking a piece of advice that could affect you in these ways (*list the outcomes you expect and specifically how those outcomes would affect them*). What would you need so you'd be okay with these changes?*

(2) Strangers. Key information can be attained from people you don't know. Search the advice-giver online to learn all you can about his/her company and reputation—look particularly for reviews, PR interviews, and anything that gives you information and insights into the advice-giver's experience, expertise, track record, clients and values. Be sure to check forums and blogs to see what advice others have received that's similar. Send out a short survey to see how your customers would respond were you to take this advice and make the recommended changes.

(3) Your mentors/coaches/consultants. Always seek perspective from the people you hire to give you advice. If you've got a solid relationship with your mentors/coaches/consultants, they will have intimate knowledge of your Journey of Impact and will be able to take into account your history, your uniqueness and your vision for the future.[76]

Hint: if the advice you're trying to decide upon originally came from them, use this language:

---

76 I have clients who text me to ask whether they should act on a piece of advice, or buy a particular product or service. It's an honor to be their lifeline at those critical moments, and I love being there for them. If you're a mentor, coach or consultant, give your clients what you wish you had when you were climbing your mountain: accessibility, clarity and opinions based on what you know about them—*not on what you would do if it were you.*

I'd like to know specifically what led you to give me this particular piece of advice. What went through your head? What are you taking into account? What do you imagine will happen if I take this advice and what do you envision if I don't?

CLEARLY DISTINGUISH OPINIONS, FACTS AND FEELINGS

OPINION: A belief, perspective, view or conviction based on what seems probable or true but not on demonstrable fact.

FACT: A thing known to be true that has actual existence.

FEELING: A physical sensation or emotion.

The key to knowing how to interpret the perspectives you receive is to make a clear distinction between **facts** and **opinions**.

While a fact is always true, opinions can vary and typically are colored by past experiences that may have little or no relation to your present situation.

If you're not sure about a perspective that's being offered to you, ask what facts are being taken into account that shaped their opinion. If the facts don't add up, the odds are the opinion won't serve you.

Once you've taken Steps 1 – 3, you're ready for a critical step in deciding which advice is best for you.[77]

STEP 4: CHECK CUSTOMIZATION

Sometimes the advice you hear comes packaged in a one-size-fits-all format that actually *could* fit for you with a little tweaking.

Say you've just published a book and you get advice to do a book tour, giving 30 book signings nationwide for the first month of your release. Cool advice, but you designed your UPtime purposefully so you'd never be gone from your family for more than three days per month.

---

[77] You'll notice there is one category missing from the list of people I'm inviting you to seek out: your friends. Unless your friends are on a similar Journey of Impact, take care in asking their advice on matters related to your business. I've learned the hard way, sometimes friends want to help, so they give advice without understanding all the facts.

So do you throw the advice away? No! You ask the advice-giver to help you figure out how to set up a virtual book tour! This small tweak will be better for your lifestyle design, more convenient for your would-be readers and the sales still count towards your bestseller status.

Just because the advice seems to be a misfit doesn't mean you can't find a way to make it fit. Get creative!

Finally, you're ready for the piece that trumps everything I've already given you. Step 5, in my opinion, is the most important of all.

STEP 5: MAKE SURE YOU'LL MINIMIZE REGRET

When I was eight years old, my mother took me to New York Memorial Hospital to see my grandfather. He was lying in bed surrounded by machines and his room was packed with people I didn't know.

As I worked my way through the crowd, strangers offered me advice like:

When you grow up, you should study math like your grandfather…

Family is everything…

Don't get too close to him, he needs his rest…

You should go out in the hall; this is no place for a child…

I was scared, but I finally got to his bed. I climbed up next to him, placed my head on his shoulder and whispered in his ear.

"Why are all these people here, Grandpa?"

"Because I made good decisions in my life, Wendel,[78] *"* he whispered back.

"How do you know if a decision is good, Grandpa?"

"Choose the one that leaves you with the least regrets."

I lifted my head to ask him to explain, but he'd fallen asleep.

---

78   This was my grandfather's special name for me. My grandmother called me "Wendala." I never liked the names when I was a kid. Now I realize what a gift they gave me.

Riding in the limo the next day, I turned to ask my mother to explain "regrets." She was fixing her lipstick and I decided to just look out the window.

There were hundreds of people at my grandfather's funeral and I wished he could come back just for a minute to tell me what he meant.

As it turned out, his advice was one of the most important lessons of my life. To this day, whenever I'm faced with a difficult decision, I simply ask myself one question:

Which choice will leave me with the least regrets?

My grandfather was a very smart man.

SO WHAT'S MY ADVICE FOR YOU?

When people come to my live events, they often ask, *Wendy, if you could only give one piece of advice to someone like me, what would it be?*

I'll tell you what I tell them:

Focus On Impact—in every area of your life.

For you, I'll take it a bit further and remind you of what I told you in the beginning of this book:

Everything you do—and everything you *don't* do—has an impact on somebody else. And when you impact just one person, that person will go on to carry your impact to the next person and the next in an endless cycle of impact.

So Focus On Impact and then make sure you're prepared to make great decisions about which advice is best for you so you can spread your impact to every life you touch.

Begin now with Action Step # 11 and then we'll go on together to the City of DARE!

ACTION STEP #11

Decide Which Advice Is Best For You

Have you ever worked with a consultant or mentor and never took the advice she or he gave you? Have you ever purchased an educational DVD or CD, E-course, webinar or downloadable information product but never got around to following through?

If so, it's time to capitalize on every penny you've ever spent on your education by practicing the steps offered in this chapter! Choose something you've purchased but never used and (Gasp!) open it up! Or find the notes from your consultation and put them in front of you.

Now, go through the **5 Steps to Decide Which Advice is Best for You** and come to a decision about how you might use the product or follow the advice that was given to you. You've got a gold mine of advice just waiting for you! Let's see where it fits!

On the other hand, if nothing fits, consider giving it to a friend or donating it to a non-profit organization. Clear your space to make room for advice that aligns with your Focus On Impact Map.

Note: If you've never purchased anything other than this book to help you grow your impact, then thank you from the bottom of my soul for choosing me to be your first guide. I take your trust very seriously and want to remind you that I'll be there for you in our online Facebook community whenever you have any questions about anything you've read here.

Once you've finished this book and completed all the Action Steps, I hope you'll venture out to see what other advice is out there waiting for you. The world is filled with people who have been there and done that - and now you're well equipped to choose the best advice for you.

The next step is to expand your impact even further in the City of DARE!

The world is waiting for your impact. Turn the page for City # 10 of your Focus On Impact Map!

Chapter Twelve

DARE TO GO BIGGER

You've captured your dream—now what?

The sun is shining brightly as you step out of your pool into the enormous towel being held open for you by the love of your life. Melting into your favorite chaise, you lean back and close your eyes, as you breathe in the warmth of this perfect day.

I did it. I really did it.

It still amazes you. Every day you receive posts, tweets, cards and emails from people you've never met, all expressing gratitude for the ways their lives have been enhanced by your message, products and services.

You've got the perfect team and you love them all for the gifts they bring to you and your company every day. Together, you've touched millions of lives, shared great adventures and generated millions of dollars—all as a result of the measurable impact you bring to each other and the people you serve.

And you? You've made more money than you ever imagined and live a life that's filled with the peace that only comes when you're doing what you were born to do.

The fear is long gone. You no longer worry about whether your bills can be paid, or your kids will be able to go to college, or your parents will receive the care they need when the time comes.

You've got everything that was on your DESIRES list and yet… truth be told, there are moments when you get a little bored.

You'd never admit it out loud, but it's just not as much *fun* anymore. You've built the mountain and arrived at the crest. And while it's more beautiful and fulfilling than you ever imagined, the challenge is gone.

Stop it! You worked hard to get here. Now sit back and enjoy the ride!

You lean over to take a sip from your favorite drink, and suddenly a jolt of electricity passes through you. You know this feeling, though it's been a while since you've felt it.

Don't you go there—you have everything you wanted—be grateful for what you've got!

Adrenalin pumps wildly through your body and you've just got to get up. You dive into the pool and move through the water as fast as your legs will take you. Lifting your head only to gulp in air, you take a deep breath and dive down to the bottom.

Flapping your hands to stay submerged, the water surrounds you in quiet bliss and it comes to you with crystal clarity.

Your new idea has arrived.

It's brilliant. It's exactly what's been missing.

YES!

You spring up to the surface, breathless with the excitement of your vision. You talk rapid-fire, sharing your new vision.

"Really? You're going to start all over again?!"

"I have to do this!"

Welcome to the intersection of Comfortable and Unknown. You've been here before. All successful journeys begin at this place. But somehow it looks different this time, because not only has your life changed, *you've* changed with it.

On the one hand, you're much more experienced. You've learned a lot on your journey and everything can be used to take you wherever you want to go next. But have you got the energy and drive to make it happen? You hear the familiar voice inside your head,

You're not getting any younger, ya know!

Tick-tock.

How do you know when enough is enough?

I get it. In fact, I'm a card-carrying frequent flyer. From the day I changed my college major to the moment I decided to write this book for you, I've launched 10 entirely different retail and service businesses, served a wide range of clients from stay-at-home moms to global leaders and created more products and services than I knew I had inside me.

And while my life has been filled with more adventures than I can recall, there were also nights when I awakened drenched with sweat, heart racing, and filled with the terror that only comes when you're caught between starting new or holding tight to the status quo.

Here's what I learned from all of this:

When you hear the call to make a new impact, It's time to brush your teeth.

In Chapter 2, I shared with you the Ritual of the Toothbrush. Every time you brush your teeth, look in the mirror and ask your reflection:

Are you making the impact you want to be making?

If the answer is yes, then before you move on to something new, do something effective to make sure you sustain the impact you're making. Because here's the simple truth of the new economy:

If you keep on doing what you've always done, you'll quickly lose what you always got!

Wait—what?!

With all respect to W. L. Bateman, Zig Ziglar, Jim Rohn and all who told us we'd keep on getting what we always got, the fact is: times have changed. In today's world, the rules of engagement shift every time a major player makes the slightest change to an algorithm. Suddenly everything you were doing that worked yesterday, stops bringing the results you expect today.

And there's more. Each time you send a new product, service, packaging, marketing piece or message out to the world, your impact is carried to far more people than the market you want to serve. You're training others who have far less creativity than you and who are more than willing to borrow your ideas! The more they compliment your genius through mimicry, the faster your innovative brilliance will be watered down in the market place.

What got you here won't keep you here.

So how do you sustain your momentum? I'll show you as soon as we look at the flip side of the coin…

Let's say you brush your teeth, look in the mirror and your answer is,

No, I'm not making the impact I want to be making!

Then it's time to do something effective by bringing your new idea to the surface.

Whenever you get a new idea, it's time to revisit the City of Define.

In the City of Define, you'll get complete clarity on your new idea by defining both your vision of impact and the measurable results it will bring for the people you serve. You'll plug your new vision into the Action Formula to be sure you have clarity on the results you want it to bring for you. And you'll take extra care to make sure you're not overlooking the DESIRES you identified the first time around.

D + R + P = ACTION

Carefully outline the full spectrum of DESIRES you want to make happen, the RESOURCES you'll need so you'll be *able* to make it happen and the PERMISSIONS you'll need so you'll be *willing* to do what it takes and let yourself have everything you want.

Then move on to the City of DISCOVER and go through the questions that led you to discover your unique gift the first time through. It's very likely you'll discover something new you hadn't seen previously, and that will give you something amazing to infuse into your new impact products and services!

Next, visit the City of DESIGN. Remember, the success of the Focus On Impact strategy depends on you loving your life *while* you build your impact. Make sure the lifestyle you created to get you here is the lifestyle you still want to live as you bring your new idea to fruition.

Of course, a new idea may mean it's time to hold a new dinner party and invite a new Table for 12. So revisit the City of DETERMINE to find the perfect market for you.

Now you're ready to create your one-of-a-kind products and services in the City of DEVELOP. Simply plug your new idea into the formula and make it happen.

Your new idea will mean a new series of impact-driven marketing, so visit the City of DIFFERENTIATE and take your team for a retreat at your favorite destination spot so you can create a new 60 Weeks of Impact and send it out to the world!

When you're ready, visit the City of DELIVER and follow the map to get people to find you, follow you, choose you, buy your offerings, use what they buy, get measurable results, send all their friends and come back for more!

Your new idea will also mean you're ready to expand your impact. So revisit the City of DIVERSIFY to reconnect with your current partners so you can alert them of your new impact. And remember: A new idea opens you up to an all-new group of collaborative partnerships. So get ready for a huge wave of synergistic energy coming your way!

As new people come into your life, so too will arrive new offers of advice to help you grow your success even further. Before you get overwhelmed, be sure to revisit the City of DECIDE to remind yourself of the steps to decide which advice is best for you.

And just when you finally get it all figured out, you'll arrive again at the City of DARE, where it will be time, once again, to pick up your toothbrush, look in the mirror and ask:

Are you making the impact you want to be making?

You see, the real power of the Focus On Impact Map is something you can only see when you look at it from way up high:

The Focus On Impact Map isn't linear—it's circular!

Contrary to traditional wisdom, going in circles assures your success!

But how do you know when enough is enough?

When you say so. And not a moment before.

Now it's time for you to do Action Step # 12, then I'll offer you some closing words to keep you going strong.

ACTION STEP #12

Dare To Go Bigger

Look at all you've accomplished. Celebrate the people you've served directly, the impact you've made in their lives, the people you've touched through them, and the dreams you've turned into reality.

Be grateful for all the people who gave you the privilege of their trust so you could serve them.

Be grateful for all those who supported you along your Journey of Impact and thank them from the bottom of your heart.

Be open to the new ideas that come to you and explore them freely with the knowledge you can do anything, as long as you follow the Focus On Impact Map, step-by-step, and come back around again and again.

And one more thing:

Every single day for the rest of your life, every time you brush your teeth, look in the mirror and ask the magic question:

Are you making the impact you want to be making?

The world is waiting for your impact. Turn the page for final thoughts on your Journey of Impact!

Chapter Thirteen

ACTION!

It's time

e've come a long way together, you and I, through 10 cities and back around again. I'm profoundly grateful you stayed with me all this way.

Now you have a decision to make. Will you put this book up on your shelf? Or will you *use* it to spread your impact as far as you want it to go and reap the rewards of the difference you bring to people's lives with your message, products and services?

You can choose to maximize and capitalize on your impact by using this book as your guide, taking Action Step by Action Step until your vision becomes a reality.

You can choose to share this book with your team, your family and your friends, so everyone understands your plan and can best support you in bringing your impact to the world.

You can choose to make this book your safety net so you always have a place to come when you get confused or overwhelmed.

You can choose to use the complimentary resources I provided for you at www.FocusOnImpact.com/resources to make the Action Steps easier and access even more resources for your success.

You can join the conversation online at www.Facebook.com/focusonimpact so you'll never be alone on your journey.

You can accept my gifts on Pages 185–190 so I can continue to serve you with proven formulas to grow your success.

Or you can choose to close this book and move on with your life.

Whatever you choose, there's something I'd love for you to know…

You have an extraordinary opportunity right now to take an action that could change your life forever.

It could also change the future for your children and your children's children for generations to come.

What action can you take that could make such a difference that it could literally change the face of our planet?

**Wake up each morning and make a decision
to make an impact on every life you touch.**

Wake up and make your impact.

Your one action will set off a ripple effect that will impact more people than you'll ever meet.

Wake up and make your impact.

In just one day, the ripple effect can take your impact around the globe and back again affecting the actions of people whose choices could determine the future of everyone around them.

Wake up and make your impact.

Your one action could move someone to be more loving, more healthy, more fulfilled, more safe and more involved.

Wake up and make your impact.

Your one action could make the difference that no one else could figure out how to make happen.

Wake up and make your impact.

It all begins with you.

All you need to do is *wake up and make your impact.*

And believe in yourself as much as I believe in you.

I honor your uniqueness. I honor the impact only you can bring our world. And I'm rooting for you more than you will ever know.

So go now and Focus On Impact.

Because the world needs your impact.

Because you need to make it happen.

And because life is far too short to settle for less than you truly want—in your business or your life.

I wish you only the very best,

Wendy

Chapter Fourteen

More Focus On Impact Success Stories

Measure your success by the number of thank you notes you receive. That's your shortest path both to the money and to a lifetime of fulfillment.

Throughout this book I've been telling you success stories and reminding you...

When you Focus On Impact, the money will come.

I'd like to introduce you now to three of my treasured clients so you can see how each has taken their unique gifts, infused them into their impact and walked the Focus On Impact Map to build their success.

Dr. Meghan McGovern helps men and women turn back the clock safely through her plastic surgery practice. When I first met Dr. McGovern, she was relatively new to private practice. Her priorities at the time were to fill her practice, pay off her medical school loans and get home early each day to her beautiful children. So when I suggested she stop thinking about money and Focus On Impact, she was understandably skeptical.

To her credit, she took a chance and launched an ongoing series of free seminars in her community—not to sell anything, but to make an impact on people's lives by providing practical information on how to understand and manage the aging process *without* the use of plastic surgery.[79]

Her practice grew quickly and as busy as she got, Dr. McGovern never lost her Focus On Impact. The more people she treated, the more she searched for unique, innovative protocols she could use to help them look natural and youthful without surgery. She ultimately discovered an innovative approach to non-surgical facelifts that has saved hundreds of people from having needless surgery. Today she trains other clinicians in her protocol and while she also offers surgical options for patients who are best suited for those interventions, her non-surgical interventions have given her a reputation around the globe for, what she calls, "*special pampering.*"

Dr. McGovern wasn't willing to settle for traditional approaches to being a surgeon. She sustains a Focus On Impact and doesn't let herself get drawn into the money side of the business. As a result, she has been highly rewarded with a beautiful home and a life that lets her spend

---

79 Today, it is very common to see physicians offering free seminars in the community, but I had my clients doing this long before it became popular. Since they were the trendsetters, the impact-driven images they set in their communities were extraordinary and the financial rewards were astoundingly huge. Today, I still encourage all my clients to share free information—locally, nationally and internationally—through Impact-Driven Marketing (see Chapter 8). The results are consistently measurable—for the people they serve, and for them!

time with her family. She loves her work, loves her patients and is a shining example of what can happen when you put money aside and Focus On Impact.

When I met **Roberto Candelaria** he had been helping non-profit organizations get sponsorship from corporations. He was young, full of energy, and classically entrepreneurial. He knew he wanted to make a bigger difference, but he didn't know exactly what he wanted it to look like.

Roberto's heart was huge and his talent was in the relationships he developed and fostered. I liked him immediately, and saw something very special in him. So when he asked me to mentor him, I was honored.

For the first few months, we focused on identifying what it was he really wanted to do. That was hard for him. He'd spent so much time focused on helping other people, it had never really occurred to him to worry about himself. At the time, all he could identify was,

"I know I want to make an impact. I know I want to speak. And I want to have the freedom to go to Disney whenever I want."

It was a place to start. In the hopes of showing him an example of how he could travel and have fun getting paid to impact people's lives, I invited him to attend a speaking engagement I was giving at a professional convention in New Orleans.

After my speech, I invited him for an iced tea. I can still see him sitting in that little area of the hotel. He was filled with dreams and his biggest challenge was the exact opposite of the audience I had just left. While they were completely focused on money, that was the furthest thing from Roberto's mind. He had no problem forgetting about the money and focusing on impact. Now the problem was getting him to let himself get *paid* for the difference he was bringing to the people he served!

Two hours later, he hugged me goodbye and walked away with crystal clarity and a plan to make it happen. In less than two years since that precious beginning, he's built a powerful impact, helping thousands of entrepreneurs capture their dreams by (1) getting funded through sponsorship and (2) getting measurable results through webinars and social networks. He holds his own live events and speaks on multiple stages serving his audiences with practical information they can use.

His rewards? A powerful community of people who adore him and consistently buy his products and services, *and* an annual pass to Disney that he liberally uses several times a year to play with friends, run marathons to benefit non-profits and eat pineapple whips in the Magic Kingdom®.

Roberto found his unique map to live the life he wants by doing what he does best: building relationships, having fun and maintaining a solid Focus On Impact.

 **Lorna DiMeo** is a board certified Clinical Social Worker, psychotherapist, world-class singer and internationally recognized healer. Unusual combination, wouldn't you agree? We met when she attended one of my live events and I was moved watching her connect with other members of my audience. Lorna is a tiny woman with an enormous presence and I watched as people were drawn to her throughout the day.

I have a tradition at my live events—I stay in the ballroom during breaks to spend time with my attendees and answer questions. I love those intimate conversations with people and my adrenalin really gets pumping as I try to make meaningful contributions for as many people as I can fit inside a short break. But when Lorna came up for her question, something was different. Rather than try to get something from me, she came to give something to me. She took my hands in her hands and thanked me. As she smiled at me, I felt as if she'd infused me with a magic elixir and my entire body spontaneously relaxed. It was quite a sensation!

I asked about her and she quickly shared her entrepreneurial journey, quietly revealing how long and hard she'd been working to find the way to get her very unique skills out to a wider audience. My heart went out to her as she described the herculean efforts and vast amounts of money she'd invested. She had learned a lot along the way, but explained how my event had, for the first time, provided the how-to details she'd been looking for. She felt hope again, and I was deeply honored when she joined my Impact Mastery program.

On our first coaching call, I discovered she had a strong background in business and psychotherapy, and had been trained extensively in Shamanic healing. I couldn't help but get a little giddy knowing I was going to have the privilege of helping an honest-to-goodness, feather-carrying Shaman get her message out to the world!

Like many baby boomer entrepreneurs, there were so many things Lorna knew how to do though she had no idea how to pull it all together into one business that would allow her to use the full breadth of her knowledge, experience and gifts.

At 67 years of age, she wanted a business that would allow her to make a huge impact while spending more time with her granddaughter and her family. She wanted the freedom to travel on her own terms, to do workshops in her community, to serve corporations, to write her book and to just BE. She'd often break into her musical laugh and remind me, *"I'm no spring chicken, honey! There's no time to waste here. If you tell me to do it, I'll do it!"*

Lorna heard her clock ticking and, like so many of her contemporaries, she was fighting the prejudicial ignorance of mainstream thinkers who assumed her methods were nothing more than *woo-woo*. So I gave her the solution that had always worked for me: research! I explained that she needed scientifically documented proof of the efficacy of the unique programs she'd created and suggested she choose three corporations in which to do pilot studies. I taught her stringent research methodologies to assess the validity, replicability and reliability of her methods. Then I helped her create research instruments to measure multiple data points before and after her interventions, with a goal of documenting tangible and perceived changes across critical areas of each team she studied.

The results of Lorna's first pilot study showed significant increases in productivity, outgoing and incoming sales, perceived teamwork and perceived levels of stress and well-being. Of particular interest was the fact that, while the team was getting more done, they perceived they were working less! The CEO was delighted and Lorna was filled with the unique pride that only documented proof can bring.

Firmly on a fast track to finally capturing her dreams, Lorna got a call that her daughter had been diagnosed with a serious health problem. There was never a moment when we questioned whether she needed to shift focus to her daughter and our entire community prayed for her and her family.

I fully expected I wouldn't hear from her for a long time, but in classic Lorna style, she not only cared tirelessly for her daughter and her granddaughter, she also kept her practice going and, whenever she had a moment to breathe, she opened her laptop to work on next steps for her new business. She never missed a coaching call, used all free time to work on her websites and her pilot studies, and never once considered she couldn't handle it all.

Today Lorna is celebrating her daughter's health, playing with her granddaughter and completing the last of her pilot studies overseas. She has a solid set of one-of-a-kind products and services for corporations and small businesses and creates customized PowerSongs™ for her clients.

Lorna never gave up—not on her daughter, not on her business, not on the people she wants to help and not on herself. And it's all paying off.

She's a role model for every transitioning professional who has questioned whether it's too late to start again, whether it's possible to care for your family while building a business or whether today's consumers will buy something that appears "woo-woo" and out-of-the-box. If that's where you are, I hope you'll think of Lorna. Because while others permit life to be their excuse, Lorna has proven over and over, life is a reason to forge ahead and Focus On Impact.

Dr. Meghan McGovern, Roberto Candelaria and Lorna DiMeo are all making their own unique and measurable impact with their messages, products and services and are being rewarded with lifestyles that are ideal for them. Is it always easy? Absolutely not. Is it always worth it? Just ask them.[80]

I'll leave you with one last success story—and it happens to have been my first.

I was four years old when I first learned to Focus On Impact. I often stayed at my grandparent's home for the weekend and whenever I was there my grandmother (quite the entrepreneur) paid me to do little jobs for her. My favorite was sharpening pencils on a contraption that was mounted on the wall in her garage.

I'd climb up on a chair, carefully place the pencil in the hole, use both hands to turn the silver handle and then pull out the pencil to inspect my work, blowing the dust from the edge. Then I'd jump down off the chair and run into the house where she inspected the pointed end. If it passed her discerning eye, she gave me a penny and a new pencil to sharpen. I loved our special routine.[81]

One summer day, my grandmother suggested I expand my "business" into the neighborhood. She gave me an empty box[82] to collect pencils to be sharpened and I spent the rest of the afternoon up in my room creating a little song for my new business. I sang it to my grandmother at dinner and she clapped her hands. I was ready!

The next morning right after breakfast, I took the little box she'd given me and we left together to walk down Tain Drive. My grandmother stayed just far enough behind me to make it feel like I was on my own as I knocked on the first door. It was all very exciting.

---

80   Connect with Dr. Meghan McGovern, Roberto Candelaria and Lorna DiMeo on our Impact Community Facebook Page at Facebook.com/focusonimpact

81   Looking back, I see now her ingenious plan to keep me busy so she could do whatever it was she needed to do!

82   I can still see the bright colors against the black background of the small box that still smelled of the Brach's candy that had long ago been inhaled by our chocolate-loving family.

A woman opened the door, and I launched into my little song, swaying back and forth as I sang my special lyrics to the tune of "*Let Me Call You Sweetheart*"[83]

> *Give me all your pencils,*
>
> *I will make them sharp*
>
> *Give me all your pencils,*
>
> *And I'll make them write*
>
> *Each one costs a penny*
>
> *For a pointy end*
>
> *Give me all your pencils,*
>
> *Aaaaaaand*
>
> *I'll be your friend.*

Okay, maybe not Grammy-Award material, but at every house they laughed and applauded and gave me pencils (one woman invited us in for cookies!). In no time, my little box was overflowing with pencils and we had to keep stopping so I could pick up those that toppled onto the sidewalk. By the time we got home my grandmother was carrying the overflow in her purse.

That afternoon I climbed up on the chair in the garage, carefully placed each pencil inside the hole and turned the little handle using both hands. I wasn't always sure how much to turn the handle, so sometimes I went too far and the point broke so I had to start again. But eventually I got them all done and proudly brought them in to show my grandmother.

She looked at each pencil very carefully and told me I had done a great job. Then she asked, *"How do you know which pencils go back to which houses?"*

---

83   Listen to Bing Crosby sing the real song here: https://www.youtube.com/watch?v=GgvDariuAN0

Huh? I had no idea which pencils went to which houses or even how many pencils each person had given me. So I did what any self-respecting 4-year-old girl would do…I cried.

Grandma responded by doing what any self-respecting grandmother would do… she gave me chocolate cake… with milk.

By the time we were done eating, Grandma had convinced me to go back to each house and explain what had happened. So we put all the sharpened pencils we could fit back into the box and the overflow in a bag that smelled like onion bagels.

As we walked up the slate steps to the first house, I could feel my knees shaking. But grandma smiled her encouragement, so I got up on my tiptoes and rang the bell. A woman opened the door and I just held out the box with both hands and blurted out,

"I did all the pencils, but I don't know which ones are yours. Can you please just pick out the ones that are yours? You don't have to pay me anything."

I must have really looked pathetic because the lady turned and went into her house, and when she came back, she gave me a dollar.

"What's this for?" I asked.

"For the song you sang for me yesterday. You brightened up my whole day! Do you think you could sing it again?"

I didn't know what to do. I turned around to my grandmother and she took the box from me and told me to go ahead. So I took a deep breath and I sang my little heart out right there on the stoop.

The nice woman gave me a second dollar and then she took my hand and marched me next door to her neighbor's house and told *her* to give me a dollar! By the end of the day the box was empty and I had $17.

My first entrepreneurial success story.

Many years later, the woman from that first house came to my grandmother's funeral. I didn't know her name, but I remembered her warm smile. She gave me a big hug as she was leaving and whispered,

"I still remember the day you and Ruthie came to my house and you sang your little song. Ruthie was so proud of her little Wendala."

Once again, I cried.

I learned a lot about entrepreneurial success from my grandmother:

✓ Be fair
✓ Do something to make an impact
✓ Keep your promises (if you can't do what you promised, be honest).
✓ When you Focus On Impact, the money will come
✓ Always keep track of your pencils

My grandmother taught me a lot about business. But more than anything else, she taught me to value impact. And I've been passing that message on ever since.

There are no limits to what you can build when you Focus On Impact. It all begins with Action Step # 1. Start now. The world is waiting for your impact!

Lessons, Gifts & Gratitude

No one makes a global impact alone.

As you look back on your life, who are the people who helped you, inspired you and infused you with information, insights and skills that shaped your impact? What lessons did you learn from those people and what gifts did they bring to your life? Who is supporting you today and helping you bring your impact to the world?

When is the last time you expressed your gratitude to all who have helped you along your Journey of Impact?

In this section, I'm going to introduce you to some of the extraordinary people who helped shape my impact and share some of the gifts and lessons they brought to my life. Some have passed on, others are very much a part of my life today, and all are indirectly impacting your life through mine. That's the ultimate power of impact. One touching one touching one in an endless cycle of impact…

THE BEGINNING...

In my first semester of college, I lived in an apartment with three roommates who bullied me on a daily basis. Despite my efforts to ignore them, their harassment escalated further each week, with threats of violence if I told anyone about their behaviors. It was a tough way to begin college, but I got through it and by the time the semester ended, I was really glad to go home.

On the final night of my holiday break, my mother found me crying in my room. She took me in her arms as I sobbed away four months of terror and humiliation. When I'd finally calmed down enough to speak, I revealed my secret and begged her not to tell anyone.

My mother sat back, handed me a tissue and shared the lesson that ultimately defined my life:

"Wendy, if you don't like it, change it."

Empowered with the knowledge that I could effect change, I returned to school, solved the problem and have lived by her words ever since. Every business I've built has been founded following the discovery of something I didn't like that I believed I could change. That's why this book is in your hands—because I don't like the idea that there could be someone out there who *needs* you and hasn't been served by you. It is a privilege to pass my mom's impact on to you.

Happily ensconced in a new apartment with my wonderful new roommate, I was now free to be inspired by the extraordinary teacher who showed me the path I walk to this day. **Dr. Eugene Fappiano** bounded into the amphitheater and welcomed us to Sociology 101 and by the end of the class, I had found a new home. His impassioned style of imparting knowledge gave me answers to questions I never knew I had. I became driven to learn more about groups, cultures and the influence society had on our lives. *Dr. Fappiano, thank you for revealing to me the science that enabled me to step up and make my impact.*

After Dr. Fappiano introduced me to sociology, he introduced me to **Dr. Alan C. Kerckhoff** the author of *Socialization and Social Change*. As my mentor in the Duke University Graduate Department of Sociology, Dr. Kerckhoff taught me to think as a social scientist and drove me to a level of excellence far beyond anything I'd imagined possible. He taught me the value of researching social problems and infused in me a deep respect for data-driven proof that I've used ever since. *Your impact led me to become a research snob, and I'll be eternally grateful for the standards you challenged me to meet. Rest in peace, Al.*

I would not be where I am today without my dear friend and colleague, **Dr. M. Dwayne Smith**. Our friendship began when we were students at Duke and grew into an exciting colleagueship in the years that followed. Working until all hours in our respective cubicles, surrounded by stacks of computer punch cards, reams of green-and-white lined printouts and the musty odor of century-old buildings, Dr. Smith was the first to encourage me to publish my research in social science journals and to present my findings at conferences. From attending classes to co-authoring journal articles, he helped me laugh through the stress, introduced me to hushpuppies and radiator caps and ultimately helped me decide to accept the game-changing invitation to leave Duke and manage the research project that forever changed my path. *Dwayno, your impact is with me to this day, in far greater depths than I can express. Thank you, my friend.*

My impact grew exponentially thanks to the grace shown to me by **Tom Hopkins**. Sales Champions worldwide respect Mr. Hopkins for breaking down the sales process into practical, implementable steps they can take to increase their impact through selling. For me, his impact went much deeper. I had the privilege of knowing his tremendous heart and vision through a conversation that forever changed my life in a tiny restaurant in Parsippany, NJ where he identified the uniqueness of my sales formulas and inspired me to pursue my dream of making my impact through training and consulting. That was nearly 30 years ago, yet I still share his story of influence at all my live events. *Thank you Tommy. I'm so deeply grateful for the impact you made in my life and in all the lives you've touched.*

As you saw in the City of DISCOVER, it isn't easy to identify your own uniqueness. So after Tom Hopkins expressed his opinion about my uniqueness, I needed to know more. I went straight to **Juanell Teague**, the brilliant woman who represented celebrity speakers such as Dr. Norman Vincent Peale, Dr. Denis Waitley, Art Linkletter and Zig Ziglar. Ms. Teague helped me see precisely how my impact was different and gave me the extreme honor of labeling me, *"The new direction in the selling industry." Juanell, your impact made it possible for me to know what I couldn't possibly have seen without you. Thank you for your wisdom, your perspective and your powerful gift!*

When I started offering training programs, I was driven to make sure my impact would last long after the trainees went home. Since I was new to training, I didn't have products or services to offer, so I purchased a franchise from **Paul J. Meyer's Success Motivation Institute** and included their products in my training contracts. This "multi-level marketing" company gave me more than a product to sell—it provided me with a laboratory to use my formulas to build and grow my own team of sales professionals. We quickly achieved the position of #1 U.S. Sales Leader and I was invited to speak to the international audience of SMI franchisees. That evening at the gala, I had the opportunity to thank Mr. Meyer. His gracious response inspired me to dare to go bigger, *"Your impact is different than any I've ever seen. The world is already better because of what you did here today."* Since that night I've had the honor of speaking on thousands of platforms around the globe, and wherever I go, I always think of Paul J. Meyer. *The world is a better place because of you, Paul. Thank you for your profound impact. Rest in peace.*

After my mom died, I was filled with a burning desire to spread my impact quickly and **Fred Pryor Seminars** was my answer. I spent three years traveling the world, teaching seminars for thousands of men and women per month. The experience I gained was invaluable, and the new sales and training formulas I developed during that time still help me make my impact today. In addition to the deeply moving experience of working with Fred himself, there were four women who had an enormous impact on me, personally and professionally. *Marsha Petrie Sue, Rhonda Scharf, Dondi Scumaci and Sharon Baker, thank you for your friendship, colleagueship and cooperative spirit. Together our impact was extraordinary.*

There aren't enough words to express the gratitude I feel for **Dr. Gary Saretsky.** It was his vision that drove me to create an entire suite of new programs for healthcare organizations. Dr. Saretsky brought my company into hospitals, medical, dental and wellness practices and onto stages worldwide. Thousands of doctors and their staff are making a significantly greater impact on patients' lives because of the risks he took sponsoring my company to serve them. *Your impact was exponential, Gary—for our mutual clients, the patients they served, my company, my family and me personally. Thank you, my dear friend.*

Nancy Collins, President of Greenbranch Publishing, changed my life. Her commitment to bringing quality information to doctors and healthcare administrators, combined with her tremendous commitment to partner with her authors, helped me make a measurable and lasting impact across the United States and Canada. Her invitation to publish my work in the *Journal of Medical Practice Management* was a game-changer for me and her subsequent invitation to publish a book with me led to my bestselling healthcare guidebook, *M.A.D. Leadership for Healthcare.* A staunch supporter of her authors, Nancy frequently recommended me for speaking engagements, providing a powerful platform for my impact. Her friendship and integrity helped me navigate a complex world and her support helped me serve in ways I never could have accomplished without her. *Nancy, you are a one-of-a-kind woman, a powerful beacon for doctors and administrators and a treasured gift in my life. Thank you.*

Some of my greatest lessons and gifts came from **Karen Sweeters,** Owner of KBSearch Company, Master Director and Certified Judge for the 501c Sweet Adelines International. What began as two women who shared a love for singing grew into so much more. Working together on several projects for the 501c Harmony on the Sound Chapter of Sweet Adelines International, we generated ideas that were far more impactful than we could ever have created alone. My tenure on her Music Leadership Team, and my years serving as President and Team Coordinator for her Management Team brought countless opportunities to develop new programs and institute a culture change that made a huge impact for our members. Those years had a lasting impact on much of what I do today for my non-profit clients and the friendship we developed along the way is one of the greatest gifts of my life. *Karen, thank you for that very first bagel and for all the gifts of trust, joy and wisdom that followed during our froyo-save-the-world dates, psych 501 brainstorming sessions, and laughter-filled conversations. You've touched my life in so many ways and I'm deeply grateful for the love we share.*

The first time I met **Rick Frishman**, I was blown away by his unique combination of heart, talent and business savvy. Within two minutes of our first hello, he smiled and said, "*We should do something together!*" Ever since that day, we've collaborated on numerous projects in the service of difference-makers. I've watched Rick make his impact on hundreds of authors' lives with his tremendous wit and massive knowledge in the publishing and PR industries. I've been privileged to serve on his Author 101 University stage on multiple occasions and together we've produced two international bestselling books, helping 34 authors collaborate to bring their impact to the world. Rick and his fabulous wife, **Robbi** have been a huge gift in my life on so many levels. *Thank you both for your friendship, your trust, your partnership and all the wisdom you provided as we worked together to make a measurable impact in a difficult industry. I treasure you.*

Gail Kingsbury came into my life when I invited her to be a judge for a speaking contest on a cruise adventure I'd created for my speaking clients. Since then, the hours we've spent together have been filled with laughter, brainstorming and impact. Gail's contact list is a who's who of world influencers, and yet her humility is second to none. Her unique perspective on the personal and professional development industry has been invaluable to me and the trust she's shown me in seeking my counsel has honored me deeply. Among the many skills she's mastered, I've been most moved by how she has mastered the balance of motherhood and entrepreneurial service. She is a role model for impact-driven women. *Gail, I'm deeply grateful for all we've shared together, but most particularly for the gift of witnessing you mother your girls into becoming the amazing women they are. I love you, sweet Gail.*

Leslie Knight has brought a special friendship and support to my life. Her keen eye for detail, calm-under-pressure leadership style, commitment to integrity, unique perspectives and quirky sense of humor have combined to make a measurable impact in my life. The world is a safer place because of Leslie and the gifts she brings to people's lives. *Les, thank you for every moment of wisdom, chocolate and spiders you've brought to my life. You're a quiet strength and I'm deeply grateful for our friendship. I love you, Les.*

My amazing team…I have impossibly high standards—particularly when it comes to serving my clients. Nevertheless, if people are going to take time away from their families to read my books, my posts, watch my videos, come to my live events and put their dreams and businesses into my hands, it's critically important to me that every detail be managed to perfection. My impact would not be what it has been without the team of men and women who manage all the details to help me bring my impact to the world:

Chase Rogers of Chase New Media has been creating and managing my online presence for more than a decade. His loyalty, creativity, patience, flexibility and there-when-I-need-him commitment has meant more to me than I can ever express. *Chase, you have my undying gratitude for all you've done—and continue to do—to keep me sane in a world of ever-changing technology and to make sure I stay connected to my community. "Thank you" will never be enough.*

I put my live events in the capable hands of **Audrey Hagen** of Platinum Events Live. Together with her fabulous team, LA Davis and Jamie Beeso, Audrey brings the perfect combination of attention to detail and heart-driven customer service that helps me consistently deliver the experiences I want for my live event attendees. Behind the scenes, Audrey has made a huge impact in my life with her wisdom, unique perspective and extraordinary sense of humor. More than a skilled professional, she's been the angel who makes even my most impossible visions come to light. *Audrey, thank you so much for your brilliance, your heart, your extraordinary ability to turn YIKES into AWESOME and for every moment of joy you bring to my life! I love you, my Blonde Sista!*

Brian Spark of Tayside Productions designs and implements the audio/visual experience at all my live events. He and his team have an unfailing ability to make sounds crystal clear, visuals shine, and audience questions heard. The magic of Tayside Productions doesn't come from the equipment they bring or the power that surges through the wires they tape around the ballroom. What drives their impeccable results is Brian's tremendous heart and perfectly timed humor. He brings me his unique roll-on-the-floor-keep-the-make-up-from-running-down-my-face experience without missing a beat of the important details of the event. *Thanks for all you do to help me help others HWB! You're one of a kind and I'm so grateful you're in my life!*

Carleton Torpin serves as director and editor for all my online videos, helping me make an intimate one-to-many impact. His unique talent for balancing what's possible with what I want consistently yields viewer experiences that turn my vision into measurable impact. His creative eye and command of technology assures his artistry supports but never upstages my message and training content—and that is simply extraordinary.[84] *Carleton, I so appreciate your patience, brilliant humor and consistent dependability. Thank you for all you bring to my life and for the thousands of texts that have gone back and forth at 2:00 a.m.!*

FINALLY, HUGE GRATITUDE TO THE PEOPLE WHO DIRECTLY INFLUENCED THIS BOOK:

I don't know when (or even if) I would have written this book if not for **Berny Dohrmann** and the invitation he gave me to serve on the faculty of *CEO Space International.* Berny's vision to create an entrepreneurial growth community based on a firm foundation of cooperation was a direct fit with my collaborative impact model and his willingness to permit me to openly research CEO Space members is precisely what led to my decision to share my Focus On Impact Map—first on his stage and ultimately here in this book. *Thank you for your vision, your deeply-felt passion to serve and the support you showed me as I brought this model to the world. And special thanks to September Dohrmann for all the details you handle that make it possible for me to help your members in such a well-managed home. You've both become precious family to me*

---

84   If you haven't yet viewed the complimentary online training course that came with your purchase of this book, be sure to grab it now at FocusOnImpact.com/resources

and I'm deeply grateful you're in my life. I love you both. How can it get better than this?

David Hancock, founder of Morgan James Publishing, graced me with his trust in publishing this book and lent his magnificent entrepreneurial vision and expertise to the distribution that brought this book to you. David's commitment to entrepreneurs, his passion for business and his strong ethical foundation of service combine to create a safe haven for impact-driven authors unlike any available today. Thanks to David's heart, a portion of the proceeds for this book will go to serve the great work done by Habitat for Humanity and I'm honored to be able to participate in his mission to give back. I'm also grateful to David's fabulous team, the eclectic, talented group of caring men and women who have been such a gift to me during the publication of all three of the books we've done together. *Thank you Margo, Bethany, Jim, Kim and especially David for all the tremendous support you've given me as we brought Focus On Impact to the world!*

My special thanks to **Cheryl Snapp Conner** of Snapp Conner PR for her enthusiastic encouragement, market wisdom and brilliant creativity in spreading the Focus On Impact message to the Forbes Online Community and beyond. *Thank you for all your help and for the beautiful, loving friendship that has emerged from our collaboration. I so appreciate you, Cheryl, am honored by your support and am excited about all the impact we're creating together! I love you, my sweet friend.*

Scott Hoffman of Folio Literary Management lent his brilliant expertise in the brain-twisting process of identifying the subtitle for this book. Scott's expertise as a top literary agent (and classic New Yorker), were invaluable to me and his insights regarding the unique contribution the book would bring to entrepreneurs was instrumental in my decision to make this book happen. *Thanks for encouraging me to write this book and for all the late-night emails that helped me think it through. I appreciate you Scott and am deeply grateful you're in my life!*

George Foster of Foster Covers is the creative genius behind the cover design of this book. George is my go-to for all my book and product cover designs. His extraordinary creativity and determination to find just the right visual for the author's message is second to none. *Thank you for your undying patience, and for your exquisite talent that consistently enables you to transform my message into a piece of art that speaks without words. Much love to you, my friend.*

Tim Boden, editor extraordinaire, made sure my writing was consistent and readable, that my intention came through with clarity and precision, and that my personal voice was never cast aside in favor of perfection. *Thank you for your insights, friendship and expertise, and for all the time you gave this project when it would have been understandable for you to place your attention elsewhere. Tim, I'm truly grateful to you.*

When **Roberto Candelaria** heard about my Focus On Impact Map and my intention to publish it as a book, he offered to take on a major role in its release. Roberto's belief in my message, his never-ending encouragement and cheerleading, his mastery of social platforms and his expansive expertise in serving non-profit organizations were instrumental at every step of the process in bringing this book to you. His friendship and support made the rough patches laughable and the exciting victories worthy of Disney fireworks. There simply aren't enough words to express my gratitude. *Roberto, thank you from the bottom of my heart for all you've brought to my life through your trust, your heart, your skills and your commitment to impact. You are family and we will always be here for you, with love, laughter and Chinese take-out.*

If you found this book on Twitter, it is likely because of **Warren Carlyle**, his boundless heart, and his insatiable hunger for social impact. I met Warren through Roberto and instantly brought him into our family. His excitement in reading this manuscript and sharing it with you was a huge gift to me. *Thanks for all the research and heart you brought to helping me take Focus On Impact social and for the special love you've added to our family.*

At the risk of sounding like a huge cliché, the Focus On Impact strategic map exists only because **countless men and women** have put their dreams and trust in my hands for over three decades. From clients who have trusted me with their entire teams to the people who read (and engage with) my emails, tweets and posts…from my cherished private coaching clients to the global audience who comments on my complimentary videos… from the meeting planners who invited me to speak to the media hosts who invited me to serve…

I am profoundly grateful to everyone who has given me the privilege of joining you on your Journey of Impact. Without you, none of this would matter.

AND FINALLY, MY SCARECROW…

In the *Wizard of Oz*, Dorothy saves the Scarecrow for last—because his impact was most precious to her. My scarecrow is **Dr. Hal Dibner**.

Since 1985, Hal has been my closest friend and *"secret weapon."* His brilliant mind, limitless heart, boundless curiosity and comprehensive education combined to make my impact richer and more life-changing than I could have ever accomplished alone.

Hal is a master of perfectly-crafted and exquisitely-timed questions that make an immediate and permanent impact in people's lives. The broad range of sciences he taught me, the insights he shared, his support during my psychotherapy training and his invitation to join him in practice all combined to impact my business and my life in countless ways.

Despite all he's taught me over more than three decades of working together, I've never come close to the precision impact Hal can make in a simple conversation. A one-man barrier-buster, Hal has helped thousands of my clients break free from the personal issues that were blocking their success. He is a brilliant diagnostician who consistently discovers the one piece that everyone else missed and helps people break through with kindness and precision.

Our partnership has afforded me the unthinkable luxury of challenging my clients to go beyond their vision of themselves, because I always knew Hal would be there to keep them safe. Together our impact has been magical and the adventures we've shared consistently amaze me.

It's impossible to express the depth and breadth of gratitude I feel being partners with a man I so deeply respect. Hal has always been focused on impact, and is the greatest difference-maker I've ever known. The fact that my business partner is also my best friend, my husband, my hero, and the love of my life is a gift that amazes me every day.

Since the first day we met, Hal has supported my dreams, encouraged my vision, cleared my path and held me up when I felt lost. When I'm vulnerable, he is my strength and when I'm strong he applauds my fortitude—that is nothing short of spectacular.

There is no greater gift than the impact Dr. Hal Dibner has made in my life, and no greater love than the one we share. *I love you Dib—with all my soul and might and everything in between. You're my hero, and I'm so deeply grateful you've shared your life with me. Here's to our next 30 years and all the lives we'll touch together!*

The true power of impact rests in the people you meet and keep in your life. I've been incredibly fortunate to have extraordinary people in my life. And now you're here too! I'm so glad you're with me!

The impact we'll make together will be far greater than any we will ever make alone.

Now it's your turn. Show your gratitude to all who have impacted your life by passing their impact on to every life you touch.

More Praise for Focus On Impact®

"I often hear executives share that one of their most difficult decisions these days is what to read and what to throw away. In my opinion, *Focus On Impact* is a must read for every executive who wants to make a difference in the lives s/he touches every day. This work provides the tools, strategies, and a roadmap that enable business leaders to create and provide products and services that impact their customers and clients in unique and special ways—and in the process of focusing on others, build a business and personal life that exceeds their dreams. I am one of many, many people who have the privilege of considering Wendy Lipton-Dibner to be a friend, and all of us enjoy spending time with this extraordinary woman and author. She always impacts our lives in positive ways! I have the book; I've read the book; now I must implement it in my life and in my business!"

— **Harry P. Lay, CPA, CPEC**, President,
Lay Professional Services, Inc.

"The beautifully presented information in *Focus On Impact* creates life changing Kairos moments of clarity. I predict it will become a beloved and well-worn difference-making reference book in most every reader's library."

— **Ellen Troyer**, CEO, Biosyntrx, Inc., Biosyntrx.com

"Wendy's honest conversational voice makes the entire experience seem like a VIP one-on-one consultation. In an incredibly short amount of time, the compounding rewards of focusing on impact become crystal clear. The stories are inspiring, the action plans both challenging and rewarding, and there are tons of great free extra resources, my favorite being the online community of like-minded Impacters who are all in your corner. Wendy equips you with the tools to be a Difference-Maker! As a business partner of Wendy's for several years related to her Live Events, I now know how she so easily fills a ballroom wall-to-wall with clients who are committed to making an impact."

— **Dennis Nemchek,** Group Sales Manager, Sheraton Stamford Hotel

"Wendy Lipton-Dibner's *Focus On Impact* is a must-read for ALL physicians. The strategies in this book helped me grow a thriving practice and live the lifestyle that's right for my family. As physicians, we tend to be afraid of coming off like used car salesmen, so we don't always give patients all the information about how we can help them. Wendy helped me realize this was keeping me from giving patients the opportunity to get what they really wanted, and I now am able to serve them in a way that genuinely impacts their lives."

— **Dr. Meghan McGovern, MD,** DrMeghanMcGovern.com

"What I love most about Wendy Lipton-Dibner's *Focus On Impact* is that it's a soup-to-nuts guide that helps us build and grow businesses that make a difference while living the life we want to live. Whether you're a Mompreneur like me, or a Fortune 100 executive, this is a model you can use to achieve business success while making the broadest positive impact."

— **Aviva Goldfarb,** CEO, The Six O'Clock Scramble and AvivaGoldfarb.com

"Get, read and study *Focus On Impact*. This is your best step-by-step guidebook to an abundant life. Wendy's meticulous map of proven strategies is the secret to living your passion. You need to read this book or miss out on the chance for a fulfilling career and the legacy of a life well lived. Don't miss a step."

— M. Constance B. Greeley, DDS

"This is not just another business success book. Every once in a while something comes along so important, so substantive, so actionable, it's better described as a goldmine than a book. You hold such a treasure in your hands. Wendy has been called, 'the next Zig Ziglar' because she exemplifies helping people get everything they want by teaching them how to truly impact other people's lives. Most people will read only one book this year; it should be this one. Read it again and again. I will."

— **Steven Sanchez**, international bestselling author, speaker, internet developer and marketer, StevenSanchez.com

"*Focus On Impact* delivers on its promise. It does so because the book itself practices what Wendy preaches. There is nothing in this book that wastes time—even the acknowledgments at the end are instructive and teach by example. The conversational style of the narrative gives you the benefit of a one-on-one connection with Wendy, which you should seek out if you can. I would put this book in the top 5% of all non-fiction that I have ever read (I am a voracious reader and also write for a living)."

— **Jason Webb, JD,** registered patent Attorney, JPWebb.us

"From right where you are, Wendy's book, *Focus On Impact* is a masterful tool for life's journey. Even if she's never met you, you'll feel like she has, because her knowledge, insight and direction provides the perfect inner-core GPS instructions to effectively guide you on your personal journey for success; whether an entrepreneur, mom-preneur, small-business owner, nonprofit, clergy, or grass-roots organization."

— **Sherita J. Herring**, business strategist and nonprofit/grants expert

"No matter how accomplished they are, *Focus On Impact* can support every entrepreneur in finding and overcoming the obstacles that prevent them from moving to their next level of success."

— **Karen Leland**, author, *Entrepreneur Magazine's Ultimate Guide to Pinterest for Business*

"What a wonderful gift Wendy Lipton-Dibner has shared with us all with her new book *Focus On Impact*. Wendy is one of those rare individuals who can seamlessly combine great storytelling with a specific step-by-step formula that will help you to achieve greater success. As you focus on the impact you want to make on the world, follow Wendy's expert guidance every step of the way. *Focus On Impact* will become one of the greatest resources in your library and you'll be referring to it again and again and again."

— **Bret Ridgway** author, speaker, co-founder
of Speaker Fulfillment Services

"If you are a difference-maker who wants to make an impact on every life you touch, then you now hold the roadmap in your hands. Wendy Lipton-Dibner has written your step-by-step guide to success in *Focus On Impact*. With honesty and transparency, Wendy shares her journey of discovery that led her to create this comprehensive and proven process that works in any economy and in any industry with remarkable results. I encourage you as the reader to see this book as the true and generous gift that it is and apply Wendy's wisdom to your life and your business and you will learn the profound joy of living a life of impact. The world is waiting for your impact—are you ready to begin your journey? Wendy will be with you every step of the way!"

—**Gail Brown**, Founder & President,
Engaging Speakers, EngagingSpeakers.com

"*Focus On Impact* is the first book on strategy in the last 10 years to reveal not only what to do, but most importantly *how* to use the strategies to build a business. Not just any business, but one that honors your desire for impact and integrity while making money. Better than *Blue Ocean Strategy*, Wendy Lipton-Dibner does not leave anything to chance. She lays it all out for you in practical action steps. All you have to do is download the free resources, follow the map and take action. When you are ready to expand your impact simply repeat the process that produces predictable results. This is a book that you will use over and over again. I highly recommend *Focus On Impact* for the impact-driven professional or entrepreneur in any business of any size at any stage of development."

— **Leslie Knight**, Founder, Custom Business Success

"Whether you're an employee, entrepreneur, just starting out, multi-million dollar brand or anywhere in between, Wendy Lipton-Dibner's *Focus On Impact* gives you what you need to serve people, align your team, make an impact and make money. I wish I'd had this book years ago. It would have saved me a lot of time and money. I love this book. It puts an end to 'trial and error.'"

— **Roberto Candelaria**, Founder, Sponsorship Boot Camp

"As a trailblazer in the national non-profit world, I have always looked for some kind of map that would give me direction to make the greatest impact I can on women battling cancer around the world. *Focus On Impact* is that MAP! This book is insightful and easy to read. Wendy shares her real-world experiences that give trailblazers like me the direction we need to make the impact on this world that we want! Thank you Wendy!"

— **Kim Becker**, Co-Founder, Hello Gorgeous! of HOPE, Inc.

"*Focus On Impact* is so timely. Wendy Lipton-Dibner is a genius at explaining our impact, and how to implement it with plenty of easy to follow examples. I love how she integrates the people that impact her life into the book, further demonstrating that impact impacts others. Read this book and get copies for your team!"

— **Ken Rochon, Jr.**, The Umbrella Syndicate

"Wendy takes an empowering and no nonsense approach to building your business and to building the business of your life! Her clear, practical and easy-to-follow advice helps to step you over the potential obstacles and keeps you on track to creating success and impact in your field. This is a book that deserves to be read!"

— **Dr. Jane Cox**, human behaviors specialist, speaker, trainer and consultant DrJaneCox.co.uk

"If you are a difference-maker or dream of being one in absolutely any area including your personal life then this book is exactly what you need. Wendy Lipton-Dibner has written the complete roadmap to taking action and becoming a difference-maker in your desired field. *Focus On Impact* not only takes you simply through the steps, it guides you easily through everything you need to create massive success by breaking the traditional business molds that have been holding us back for so long. Wendy says to "Never underestimate the power of your impact" and that is so true. Her experience in moving people to action shows throughout this brilliant book."

—**Gail Kingsbury**, Founder, *Real Wisdom TV*
and the Gail Kingsbury Group

"Once again Wendy Lipton-Dibner shows her brilliance and her mastery! Her book *Focus On Impact* is so exciting because it's easy to read, clear and concise. She gives you a step-by-step map that tells you exactly what to do to get what you want, exactly the way you want it. So if you're just beginning your journey or well along your way, *Focus On Impact* will have something for you. This book is a must-read for everyone who wants to create the life of their dreams!"

— **Lorna DiMeo, MSW**, Success On Purpose, Inc.,
FreePowerSong.com

"Ready to meet your impactful self? Then allow Wendy Lipton-Dibner to facilitate the introduction. Lipton-Dibner's impact is her ability to show you how to discover, distinguish and deliver your uniqueness onto a world that sorely needs you. She's been live-teaching her curriculum to groups for decades, but now her organized, time-tested, scientifically backed Action Formula and action steps are available, for the first time ever, in an amazing book: her just-released *Focus On Impact*. Lipton-Dibner asks probing questions; she challenges you; she coaches you; she lifts you out of fears. She generously shares her vast business and marketing experience, making it easy for you to roll back the fog and unleash the wonderful, real, impact-driven you. Read her book, and then go for it, because she is giving you the gift of you. There's never been a more wonderfully organized way to plan your future, your career and your life."

— **Patty Soffer** #1 international bestselling author,
small business coach & brand strategist, PattySoffer.com

"*Focus On Impact* is a masterpiece of brilliance for succeeding in today's economy. Wendy Lipton-Dibner proves once again that she is committed to impact and she walks her talk with specific steps and actions to be successful. Following Wendy's advice can truly result in living the life of your dreams. The reader will find this book to be a groundbreaking experience."
— **Barry Laub**, CFP, international bestselling author, BarryLaub.com

"Do you have a sense of the incredible positive impact you could be having in the world? Well guess what—it's a lot more than you think! Wendy does a fantastic job of helping you see the possibilities in your greatness, and most importantly, provides a fantastic step-by-step plan to help you define, expand, plan, and realize your potential. Get the book, implement the action steps, and make your impact—you will be glad you did!"
— **Paul Hoyt**, business consultant and bestselling author

"Wendy Lipton-Dibner has a knack for being able to reverse engineer her and others' success and then to teach it to you so you know what to do, how to do it, AND give you the tools to get it done. In *Focus On Impact*, she captures her live coaching style with an elegance that you feel Wendy jump off the page. It is my fervent wish that you too get to work personally with Wendy. But until that time, this book lets you experience her mastery for yourself so you can make your biggest impact."
— **Dr. A. Kumar Ramlall, MD, FRCPC, FAAP, FCCP**,
Co-Founder, Chintan Project, Founder, InspiroMed Clinics,
Clinical Associate Professor, University of Alberta

"#1 International Bestselling Author, Wendy Lipton-Dibner, does it once again with a book that is nothing short of inspiring, thought-provoking and absolutely brilliant! *Focus On Impact* is one of those rare treasures that will make you wish you had gotten your hands on a copy sooner. Wendy is not only the original advocate but also the world's greatest cheerleader for anyone interested in making a true impact on the world. For the first time in print, Wendy details her *Focus On Impact* Map which is a step-by-step comprehensive model that will teach you how to reset your mindset and trust it to work for you by harnessing your power to impact people's lives. When you follow Wendy's map, you will quickly be on the road to wealth AND a life by design—All while making a measurable impact on every life you touch. This book is for anyone focused on making a difference, but be warned... once you crack the spine, you will not want to set it down!"

— **Pat Skiffington**, international bestselling author, CEO, Keller Williams Classic Realty Group, Orlando, FL, PatSkiffington.com

" '*Focus On Impact and the money will come,*' says Wendy, who learnt by losing her say. What a blessing that was! Wendy's impact now crosses continents, as did I, to learn from this amazingly talented lady. If making a difference inspires you, take the City Tour using the *Focus On Impact* Map to discover your unique gifts. Well-designed worksheets awaken you to the essence within, showing how to live a prosperous and impactful life on purpose. Whether you're just starting out or established in business, this book will light your fire!"

— **Janet Swift** #1 international bestselling author, life dynamics coach, JanetSwift.com

"When you ask the right questions you get the answers you need to launch you and your business in the right direction. *Focus On Impact* is the definitive guide to helping you find and reach your right direction. Following the process laid out in this seminal work by Wendy Lipton-Dibner, enables anyone who is willing to do the work to achieve their goals of making a difference while living the life they design. Wendy guides the reader step by step to unlocking their unique gift and then how to launch their business into the world. I highly recommend this book. It is an invaluable resource for today, tomorrow and ten years from now."

— **Laura Steward**, business strategist, award-winning, international bestselling author, radio host, LauraSteward.com

"A must-have book if you want to make a difference! If you truly want to make a difference in your life and the lives of others, this is a 'must-have' book that you will read over and over, along with supporting 'homework' and resources you will turn to repeatedly, as you move toward your ultimate goals. Wendy is truly the 'Impresario of Impact,' and eager to teach you to make your own impact. As a psychiatrist transitioning into the world of writing and speaking, I have taken many courses, read many books and educated myself into an overload of confusion and dead ends. There are many experts out there with their particular skills they teach, but somehow that wasn't helping me get it together. Wendy, on the other hand, is dead on in the way she has put together this book as a roadmap of how to first figure out who you really want to be and what you really want to do, and then get there step by step. With a lifetime of experience making impact, she shares with warmth, humor and human understanding the path she has taken to success. The lessons she learned are now passed on to you to aid in your journey. Her approach has the simplicity one finds in true genius—boiling things down to their simplest basic fundamentals so it is easy to grasp them and build on them…With Wendy guiding you, your journey will be limited only by your own desire and imagination, and she provides plenty of tools to help you examine those as well."

— **Judy Cook, MD**, author, *To Die or Not to Die,*
Ten Tricks to Getting Better Medical Care, GoDrJudy.com

"If you are a Difference-Maker—someone more interested in leaving your world a better place than you found it, *Focus On Impact* will provide the strategy and tactics to maximize your influence. Wendy Lipton-Dibner has drawn a detailed map and has included turn-by-turn instructions to take YOU to your destiny and turn your dreams into reality. Wendy is a veteran traveler—she's been down this road multiple times and has led many high-impact Difference-Makers on their own expeditions to success. And most remarkable of all, she generously shares her *secret* formula to anyone with the motivation to *Focus On Impact.*"

— **Timothy W. Boden, CMPE**, ClarifyYourStory.com

"I knew I was a difference-maker. My clients and colleagues tell me so. What I did not know is how I could do more, both for my clients and for myself. *Focus On Impact* is such a generous book. In her usual style, Wendy gives of herself and from the heart. Each page is a small gift. Now that I have a better understanding of what has not been working, I can focus on impacting more lives and better capitalize on my efforts."

— **Michelle A. Riklan**, Managing Director,
Riklan Resources, RiklanResources.com

"Harness the power that you know more than you think, where you are capable of far more than you know. Let Wendy teach you how to truly share your gift with the world to focus on the impact of your legacy."

— **Dr. Cheryl Lentz**, The Academic Entrepreneur

"Wendy's mastery of the human mindset, positions her as one of, if not the best, business leaders in today's market. Her IMPACT is perfection and if implemented, brings more to your life than can ever be imagined."

— **Katerina St. Claire**, international bestselling author, KaterinaStClaire.com

"As the founder of Total Image Institute, I teach women to make an impact with their clothing, body language, and speech, so the roadmap that Wendy shares in *Focus On Impact* has been instrumental in elevating my impact with the women I work with, and therefore the results that my clients experience are exponentially higher!"

— **Colleen Hammond**, Founder, Total Image Institute

"No one knows how to organize information like Wendy Lipton-Dibner. She's thorough and clear in the sharing of her decades worth of experience and knowledge so that the reader has a blueprint to follow step by step. Her emphasis on IMPACT rather than getting myopic around only bottom-line dollars breathes new life into pursuing one's passion. When your WHY is fully honored and you have the tools for creating the kind of impact you want, that's power and creates the real success. Wendy lays it all out for you here."

— **Lynn Rose**, CEO, *The WOW Factor* and *Launch You Now*, LynnRose.com

"This book is absolutely relevant and articulate in its one simple truth: '*Focus On Impact, the money will follow.*' Wendy elegantly guides you down a path, step-by-step, mapping the terrain as she goes using her own valuable life lessons in a succinct and personally revealing manner

in order to provide clear and powerful instruction on how to make your unique mark in this world."
— **Rose Sheehan**, business mentor, professional speaker, #1 international bestselling author, RoseSheehan360.com

"BRILLIANT! This book, a MUST-read for anyone with a passion to make a difference, offers practical tips to help you discover your own unique gift of impact along with a comprehensive and strategic step-by-step map to guide you on your personal journey to build a business with rippling impact beyond your wildest imagination!"
— **Babs Kangas**, PhD, Founder, freefunandfabulous.com

"*Focus On Impact* is a game-changer! If you are ready to make a difference and change lives, this is a MUST-READ! The easy to follow map provides step-by-step strategies for success in serving."
— **Cathy Alessandra**, #YESICAN Coach, CathyAlessandra.com

"You are holding a treasure map. Following the steps found in these pages will set you apart from the masses, accelerate wealth accumulation and make every day happier and more exciting. Read *Focus On Impact* and then share it with your friends. It's your time to make an impact."
— **Aaron Scott Young**, CEO Laughlin Associates, author, speaker, strategic consultant to leaders

"I thoroughly enjoyed Wendy Lipton-Dibner's new book *Focus On Impact*. This work is much more than a business plan on steroids—it is packed with information, and will serve as a reference to readers about how to 'BE' in business. Wendy shows us how to manage our impact on others in a heart-warming and eye-opening way, providing us with important glimpses into the past that directed her path. This book will help guide our path to success."
— **Andris Kazmers**, MD, MSPH, FACS

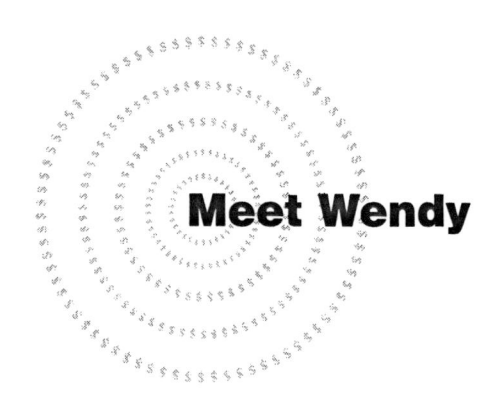

Meet Wendy

WENDY LIPTON-DIBNER, M.A. is the world's leading authority on business development through impact strategy. President of Professional Impact, Inc. and founder of the *Action Movement*™, Wendy is internationally-recognized for her unparalleled ability to help clients maximize and capitalize on the impact they bring to people's lives through their message, products and services.

Wendy serves as a trusted advisor to doctors, executives, start-up entrepreneurs and top influencers across a wide range of industries. A sought-after media guest and keynote speaker, she has built 10 successful businesses of her own, delivered thousands of business growth programs for corporate, healthcare, small business, non-profit and entrepreneurial organizations and has spoken for hundreds of thousands of people on stages around the globe.

Wendy received her Masters Degree in sociology and social psychology from Duke University and was recruited by Texas Christian University for a position as a university instructor and director of organizational research studies. One of her projects caught the eye of the United States Senate, where her presentation influenced a decision that has since helped millions of people.

Driven to make an even wider impact, Wendy left academia to open her first business: a social laboratory to develop and test formulas to move people to action. Within three months, her retail and service sales skyrocketed beyond industry standards and she became a sought-after consultant for small businesses, sharing the formulas she'd discovered for sales, leadership and customer service.

Wendy went on to achieve certification in three schools of psychology and built a private practice specializing in sales professionals. Her proprietary blend of psychotherapy, sales and leadership training helped her clients dramatically increase revenues, leading to a swell of invitations for consulting and training in for-profit and non-profit organizations where she became known for creating solid results in record time.

Since then, Wendy has impacted millions of lives through her bestselling books, live events, world-class keynotes and media appearances, online courses and in-house training programs. Her books are required reading in hospitals, medical practices, dental schools and businesses, and her work has been widely published in business, healthcare and social science journals, magazines and e-zines. Her internationally-acclaimed, *Move People to Action*™ *Live Event* and *E-Course* have been named, *"The most comprehensive training ever created for impact-driven entrepreneurs"* and her *Difference-Maker Summit*™ has been called *"The do-not-miss event for anyone who is driven to make a global impact."*

In addition to serving clients, Wendy's greatest joys are sharing laugh- 'til-you-cry experiences with cherished friends, and cozy evenings with her husband/business partner, Dr. Hal Dibner, and their fluffy son, Parfait.

To learn more about Wendy and get complimentary training for growing your impact, visit www.ProfessionalImpact.com.

CONNECT WITH WENDY:

Twitter.com/ImpactExpert

LinkedIn.com/in/WendyLiptonDibner

Facebook.com/focusonimpact

Join Wendy Live

Wendy Lipton-Dibner's
MOVE▶PEOPLE▶TO▶ACTION
Influence ▶ Impact ▶ Income

Join Wendy at her Internationally-Acclaimed
Move People to Action™ Live Event
And Discover Her Secrets to...

⇨ Build a multi-million dollar, impact through ethical influence

⇨ Get people to FIND you, FOLLOW you, CHOOSE you, SEND all their friends to your door & COME BACK for more!

⇨ Create Impact-Driven Marketing™ to make your difference and dominate your market

⇨ Get hired internationally as a highly-paid, respected keynote speaker

⇨ Develop and capitalize on bestselling books, E-courses, DVDs, CDs, podcasts, webinars & membership sites, speaking engagements, videos, teleseminars, social media and radio, TV and print interviews

⇨ Move people to click, like, share and buy without ever doing an actual sales presentation!

⇨ Make a measurable impact while living your ideal lifestyle

⇨ Get up to $150,000 for a single speech!

⇨ Get invitations from sponsors to buy and promote your books, products and services

⇨ Make a transformational impact on every life you touch with proven formulas that help people say YES to what they truly want.

And SO Much More!

IMPACT GIFT
Get the details and register with coupon code IMPACTMPTA at
www.MovePeopleToAction.com

"The best 4-day seminar I've ever attended (and I've done many)...well thoughtout information and a blueprint for how to move people to action." - Eric Bischoff

DIFFERENCE-MAKER
——SUMMIT™——
REACH MILLIONS, MAKE MILLIONS,
AND LOVE YOUR LIFE ALONG THE WAY

Join Wendy Live!

4 Days of Step-By-Step Training
Customize Your Focus On Impact® Strategic Map
Personal Coaching and "Hot Seats"
Game-Changing Networking Activities
Participate in the Global Collaboration Project™
Maximize and Capitalize on Your Impact!

IMPACT GIFT
Get the details and register with coupon code IMPACTDMS at
www.DifferenceMakerSummit.com

"Wendy Lipton-Dibner is the world's leading authority on expert collaboration! Her projects become international blockbusters."

— *Rick Frishman, Author 101 University*

Join Wendy Online

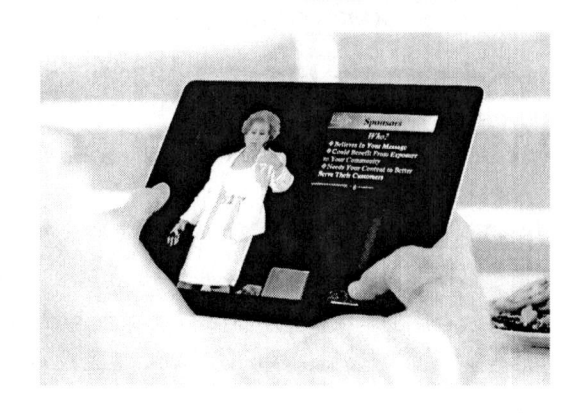

Online Course

GET WENDY'S POWERFUL STRATEGIES ANYWHERE – ANYTIME – on ANY DEVICE!

Move People to Action™ E-Course

Capitalize on your Focus On Impact® Map with the most comprehensive, step-by-step training ever created to help you use Wendy's proprietary ethical influence strategies.

Get people to FIND you, FOLLOW you, CHOOSE you, REFER to you and keep COMING BACK FOR MORE so you can grow your influence and income by making an impact on every life you touch!

IMPACT GIFT

Get the details and register with coupon code IMPACTONLINE at
www.MovePeopleToActionOnline.com

"The most content-filled conference for teaching and motivating you to effect real change in the world through your message."
- Steven Sanchez

Are You A Difference-Maker?

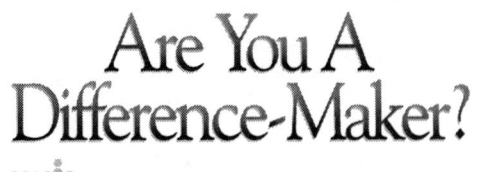 THE·ACTION·MOVEMENT™

The Action Movement™ is a powerful community of speakers, authors, experts, executives and entrepreneurs who have come together to create a massive global impact - one message at a time.

Discover how you can grow a fulfilling and profitable business with the collaborative support of thousands of impact-driven men and women!

For Free Training And Ongoing Support to Grow Your Income As a RESULT OF Your Impact…

Join The Movement Now!

"The impact we make together will be far greater than any we can make alone!"
– Wendy Lipton-Dibner

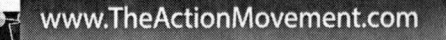

www.TheActionMovement.com

Are you ready?

Then let's tell the world you're ready to make an impact on every life you touch!

TWEET

@ImpactExpert I'm ready!

And I'll retweet!

Together our impact will be far greater than any we will ever make alone!

CPSIA information can be obtained at www.ICGtesting.com
Printed in the USA
LVOW08s2305081015

457491LV00001B/1/P

9 781630 474027